SINGER
SEWING REFERENCE LIBRARY®

Halloween Costumes

COWLES
Creative Publishing, Inc.

Minnetonka, Minnesota, USA

SINGER

SEWING REFERENCE LIBRARY®

Halloween Costumes

Contents

COWLES
Creative Publishing, Inc.

President/COO: Nino Tarantino
Executive V. P./Editor-in-Chief:
  William B. Jones

Copyright © 1997
Cowles Creative Publishing, Inc.
Formerly Cy DeCosse Incorporated
5900 Green Oak Drive
Minnetonka, Minnesota 55343
1-800-328-3895

HALLOWEEN COSTUMES

Created by: The Editors
of Cowles Creative
Publishing, Inc., in
cooperation with the
Sewing Education
Department, Singer Sewing
Company. Singer is a
trademark of The Singer
Company Limited and is
used under license.

Books available in this series:
Sewing Essentials, Sewing for the Home, Clothing Care & Repair, Sewing for Style, Sewing Specialty Fabrics, Sewing Activewear, The Perfect Fit, Timesaving Sewing, More Sewing for the Home, Tailoring, Sewing for Children, Sewing with an Overlock, 101 Sewing Secrets, Sewing Pants That Fit, Quilting by Machine, Decorative Machine Stitching, Creative Sewing Ideas, Sewing Lingerie, Sewing Projects for the Home, Sewing with Knits, More Creative Sewing Ideas, Quilt Projects by Machine, Creating Fashion Accessories, Quick & Easy Sewing Projects, Sewing for Special Occasions, Sewing for the Holidays, Quick & Easy Decorating Projects, Quilted Projects & Garments, Embellished Quilted Projects, Window Treatments, Holiday Projects, Halloween Costumes

Library of Congress Cataloging-in-Publication Data
Halloween costumes.
    p. cm. — (Singer sewing reference library)
  Includes index.
  ISBN 0-86573-316-3 (hardcover) — ISBN 0-86573-317-1 (softcover)
  1. Costumes. 2. Halloween. 3. Machine sewing. I. Series.
TT633.H347   1997
646.4'78—dc21
                           97-3875

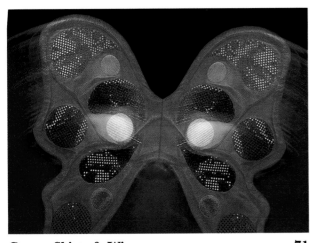

Group Executive Editor: Zoe A. Graul
Managing Editor: Elaine Johnson
Writer: Linda Neubauer
Associate Creative Director: Lisa Rosenthal
Senior Art Director: Delores Swanson
Editor: Janice Cauley
Researchers: Dawn Anderson, Valerie Hill,
  Kristi Kuhnau, Linda Neubauer
Project & Prop Stylists: Coralie Sathre,
  Joanne Wawra
Lead Samplemaker: Phyllis Galbraith
Sewing Staff: Arlene Dohrman, Phyllis
  Galbraith, Bridget Haugh, Carol Pilot,
  Michelle Skudlarek, Nancy Sundeen
Senior Technical Photo Stylist:
  Bridget Haugh
Technical Photo Stylists: Sue Jorgensen,
  Nancy Sundeen
V. P. Photography & Production: Jim Bindas
Studio Services Manager: Marcia Chambers

Photo Services Coordinator: Cheryl Neisen
Lead Photographer: Rebecca Schmitt
Contributing Photographers: Rex Irmen,
  Chuck Nields
Photography Assistant: Greg Wallace
Publishing Production Manager:
  Kim Gerber
Desktop Publishing Specialist:
  Laurie Kristensen
Production Staff: Laura Hokkanen,
  Mike Schauer, Kay Wethern
Consultants: Linda Nelson Bryan,
  Laura Emmer, Sharon Englund,
  Carol Richerts, Kathleen Richerts,
  Diane Schultz
Contributors: American Efrid, Inc.; Coats &
  Clark Inc.; Conso Products Company;
  Dritz Corporation; Dyno Merchandise
  Corporation; EZ International; Hobbs
  Bonded Fiber; HTC-Handler Textile

Corporation; Kunin Felt, Division of
Foss Manufacturing Company; Olfa®
Products International; One and Only
Creations; Plaid Enterprises, Inc.;
Putnam Company, Inc.; Snazaroo;
Sulky of America
Special thanks to the Cowles Creative
Publishing employees, families, and
friends who modeled the costumes.
Printed on American paper by:
R. R. Donnelley & Sons Co.
99 98 97 / 5 4 3 2 1

Bird creature costume elements include a full suit with a colorful design insert and shoe flaps. Felt bat-style wings and feathery wristlets and anklets give the costume flight. A customized ball cap adds unique character.

6

Introduction

Halloween festivities, from parties to trick-or-treating, always revolve around costumes. The adventure and merriment of the occasion are fueled by the creative collection of pretenders, showing off their masquerade attire. Unique and original costumes always attract the most attention, much to the amusement of the wearer. It is no wonder Halloween has become one of the busiest seasons for the home sewing industry. After all, sewing and creativity go hand in hand.

In *Halloween Costumes* you will discover ways to design and sew costumes that are uniquely yours. By breaking the total costume down into separate elements, you can build a costume that is as simple or detailed as you wish. Similar construction techniques are used for various elements throughout the book, making them very compatible.

Familiarize yourself with the costume elements from each section of this book. Also consider the amount of time you wish to invest in making the costume, as well as the expense. Time commitment and expenses can vary greatly, depending on the fabrics and embellishments selected for the costume elements.

At this point the real fun begins! Determine the costume elements from each section of this book that would best portray the animal, object, or character you desire. Use the examples shown here and on pages 8 to 13 to help you with your selections. Make a sketch of the costume, listing the details and embellishments that would make the costume uniquely yours.

Assemble all the fabrics and other materials you will need. Allow your imagination to work overtime, turning your shopping trip into entertainment. Then enjoy creating your one-of-a-kind Halloween costume, following the photographs and instructions throughout this book.

Costume Styles. Beginning with the Costume Styles section, you may choose to make the main body of the costume in one of three styles. Most costumes begin with tabards (page 19), gowns (page 33), or full suits (page 39). You will learn ways to design and personalize each of these styles.

Headwear. Another element of many costumes is worn on the head. You may wish to sew an elaborate padded hood (page 56) with eyes, ears, and horns, or perhaps a simple headband (page 64) with antennae is all that is needed for your costume. These and many other ideas can be found in the Headwear section.

Capes, Skirts & Wings. In the Capes, Skirts & Wings section, you will find basic instructions to help you design and sew many variations of each of these elements. They can be used alone or combined with elements from the other sections to enrich your costume.

Finishing Touches. Ideas and instructions for sewing original armbands, wristlets, leggings (page 105), and spats (page 115) can be found in the Finishing Touches section. Various collar styles (page 101) are also introduced. These and other easy-to-make accessories can add the details that give your costume that custom look.

Foundation Garments

Various garments are suitable to serve as the foundation of a costume. Some can be purchased inexpensively, while others can be sewn following simple instructions or by using basic patterns.

Costumes that consist of a tabard (page 19) and assorted accessories require very simple undergarments.

Depending on the climate, these may include a leotard and tights, or, for more warmth, a fleece sweatshirt and pants. Measurements for the outer costume should always be taken over these undergarments.

A gown may be the basic garment needed for a variety of costumes, such as a witch, a wizard, a princess, an angel, and many others. Any basic gown pattern can be used, or a simple gown can be folded, cut, and sewn, following the instructions on page 33. The distinguishing characteristics of the gown costume are derived from the fabric selected as well as the embellishments and accessories that are added to it.

Simple costumes for toddlers and older children can be created from purchased sleepers and a few creative embellishments and accessories. Or basic sleeper, pajama, jumpsuit, and sweat suit patterns can be modified, as on page 39, to create many costumes, from assorted animals to vegetables to wherever your imagination takes you.

Costume Examples

The examples shown here and on the following pages illustrate many combinations of costume elements that can be sewn, following the instructions in this book.

Zinnia (opposite) grew from a basic leotard and tights. A padded hood with petals blooms around her face; a leaf skirt encircles her waist; and leafy gathered wristlets, anklets, and collar complete the transformation. A whimsical dragonfly is painted on her cheek.

Jack-o'-lantern (opposite) consists of a tabard worn over a sweat suit. The leafy gathered collar, wristlets, and anklets testify to her roots in the plant kingdom.

Fairy princess (below) wears a full-overlay skirt over a leotard and tights. Sparkly padded wings, halo-style crown, and glitzy star wand feed the fantasy. Gathered collar, wristlets, and anklets give her a magical aura.

Lion costume (below), sewn from a jumpsuit pattern, boasts a terrific tail, furry tummy insert, and shoe flaps. The proud mane, attached to a padded hood, is the *purr*-fect frame for a cute face.

Witch (right) makes the Halloween scene in a hat, gown, and cape. Gloves with long green fingernails clutch her broom. Store-bought hair sets off her eerie, painted face.

(Continued on next page) 9

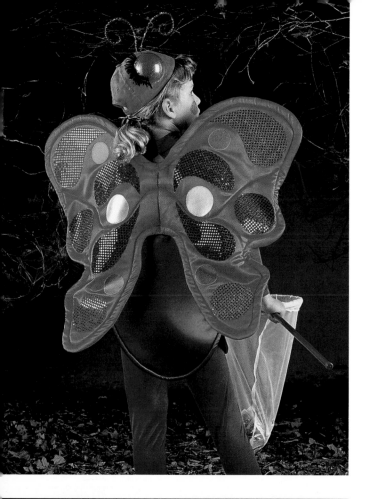

Costume Examples (continued)

Butterfly (left) flits into view, wearing appliquéd padded wings attached to a tabard. A restyled ball cap sports glossy eyes and metallic antennae. Inexpensive canvas shoes are painted to match the costume. Undergarments can be selected to suit the weather.

Dragon costume (lower left), worn over tight-fitting undergarments, includes a design-blocked tabard with shaped, spiked tail and padded wings. The padded hood has horns, ears, glossy eyes, and spikes. Claw-tipped gloves and knee-high spats reinforce the theme, while face paint enhances a ferocious expression.

Gypsy (right) whirls in her long gathered skirt, adorned at the waist with a trinket-trimmed scarf. Purchased or sewn peasant blouse, gaudy jewelry, and head scarf quickly complete the costume.

Bumblebee tabard, sewn with stinger, sheer wings, and extra legs, can be worn over any weather-wise clothing. Perky antennae and glossy eyes transform an ordinary ball cap.

Baby bee buzzes around in a design-blocked hooded sleeper with detachable sheer wings and springy antennae. How sweet!

Superhero wears sleek-fitting pants and top. Padded spats, armbands, and collar are emblazened with layered metallic appliqués. Padded headband and belt are sewn with the same techniques.

Angel floats about in a gathered-sleeve gown, adorned with decorative cord. Star-spangled padded wings are worn with an elastic harness, hidden under the gown. A shimmery halo is proof of her innocence.

(Continued on next page)

Costume Examples
(continued)

Magician wears a knee-length lined cape over plain black pants and shirt. Add a curled mustache and a hat deep enough to hide a bunny, and—*presto!*—you have a costume.

Lady-in-waiting (right), easily identified by her veiled hat, returns to medieval times in her matching gown and satin collar.

Wizard (right) conjures up Halloween fun, wearing a gown and cape. Celestial accents twinkle, from his hat to his cheeks to his glow-in-the-dark wand.

Robot costume includes a tabard dotted with gadgets, vent hose leggings and armbands, and padded spats. These elements, sewn from metallic fabrics, are worn over tight-fitting clothes. Effective details include spray-painted gloves, an aluminum pail hat, and some imaginative face painting.

Pets' costumes require some modifications. Half-circle cape allows free movement; hats are made in miniature.

The royal couple (below left), crowned and bejeweled, promenade in rich-looking capes. Her Highness wears a gathered skirt with braid-trimmed sheer overlay. Velvet ribbon woven through lace beading makes quick, elegant cuffs. The king, wearing a short, braid-trimmed gown over knickers, bears the royal scepter.

Bat costumes must have bat wings to get them flying. Worn over tight clothing, they can be attached with elastic loops. Baby bat's wings are buttoned to her sweat suit. Sew bat ears to headbands, apply face paint, and add some simple accessories.

13

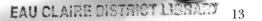

Safety & Comfort

Metallic fabrics reflect light, making the costume more visible.

Safety and comfort are important considerations when making a costume. Restrictive or oversized clothing can be uncomfortable and unsafe to wear. Tabard costumes (page 19), however, allow free movement of the arms and legs, and are both comfortable and safe. Long gown costumes (page 33) are easier to walk in if they are hemmed at the ankles. The addition of a belt helps control the fullness of a gown. Full suit costumes (page 39) fit well when they are made from pajama or sweat suit patterns.

Headwear that covers the mouth or nose can make breathing and communicating difficult. Most of all, the wearer of the costume must be able to see clearly and be seen by others. Instead of a mask, face paint (page 122) can be used to create the desired effect, while still allowing maximum range of vision for the wearer.

To increase the safety of trick-or-treat activities after dark, use light-reflective fabrics, such as metallics, whenever possible. Also consider attaching battery-operated lights to a prominent area of the costume for visual impact as well as safety.

Open-faced hoods and face paint allow the wearer clear vision and breathing, unlike masks, which often impair these functions.

Battery-operated lights and chemical-reactive lights can be worn or carried for added safety.

Glow-in-the-dark paints, reflective tapes, and stickers can increase the visibility of a costume.

Costume
Styles

Tabards

A primary element of many costumes is a tabard. It consists of front and back panels connected over the shoulders and open at the sides. A ribbon belt secured at the waist keeps the tabard in place while allowing free movement of the arms. Tabards are a great alternative to full suit costumes, as they can be made more quickly with very little consideration to fitting. Simple undergarments (page 8) are used to complete the basic costume, with the addition of any desired headgear or other accessories.

The surface of the tabard can be embellished in a variety of ways. Shapes, such as the eyes, nose, and mouth of a jack-o'-lantern, can be cut out and appliquéd (page 30) to the front or back of the tabard. Strips of jagged points can be cut from colorful felt and sewn in rows to the surface of the tabard to represent scales or feathers. Insect legs and stingers, or animal tails (page 25) can be sewn and attached to the sides or back of the tabard. Found objects, such as large buttons, metal springs, or egg cartons, can be painted and hand-sewn to the surface of the tabard, to mimic the mechanical riggings of a robot. The possibilities are limited only by the imagination.

It is always a good idea to sketch the costume before drawing the pattern. Determine what other elements to include along with the tabard to complete the costume. If there is a tail, for example, plan to make the back panel of the tabard long enough to allow for its attachment.

✂ Cutting Directions

Cut one tabard front and one tabard back from fabric. Cut one tabard front and one tabard back from lining. Cut one tabard front and one tabard back from ¼" (6 mm) foam.

Cut two 6" (15 cm) pieces of ribbon for the shoulder straps. Cut four 4" (10 cm) pieces of ribbon for the belt loops. Cut a piece of ribbon for the belt, with the length equal to the waist measurement plus 20" (51 cm) for tying.

YOU WILL NEED

Paper, for drawing the pattern.

Fabric, for front and back panels, and for self-lining, if desired.

Interfacing, for lightweight fabrics, optional.

Fabric scraps, for appliqués, optional.

Lining fabric, for panels that are not self-lined.

¼" (6 mm) foam, for tabard interlining.

⅞" (2.2 cm) grosgrain ribbon, in color to match tabard or undergarment.

How to Draw a Pattern for a Basic Tabard

1) Sketch desired tabard design. Measure width across shoulders and distance from shoulders to desired length of tabard front and back. Draw pattern in desired shape on paper, drawing gentle curve about 1" (2.5 cm) deep at neck. Add ½" (1.3 cm) seam allowance around entire pattern. Cut out pattern.

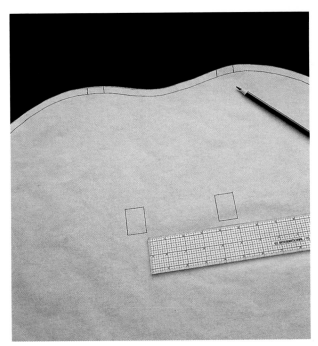

2) Hold pattern up to body. Mark desired positions for shoulder straps. Mark placement for two belt loops at waist level, spaced 3" to 5" (7.5 to 12.5 cm) apart in centers of front and back tabard patterns.

1) **Apply** any surface embellishments that should be done before construction, such as appliqués (page 30). Fold each ribbon for the belt loops in half; stitch ½" (1.3 cm) from cut ends. Press seam allowances open; press each loop flat, with seam centered.

2) **Pin** belt loops, seam side down, to right side of tabard front and back lining pieces at marks. Stitch loops to lining along upper and lower folds of loops.

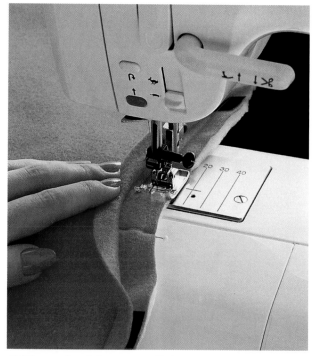

3) **Pin** shoulder straps to right side of tabard front at marks, aligning raw edges; baste. If legs are desired, make legs (page 25) and baste to right side of tabard front along outer edge.

4) **Place** tabard front over lining, right sides together; layer, lining side down, over the foam. Pin. Stitch ½" (1.3 cm) from raw edges around the entire tabard, leaving opening between shoulder strap marks for turning. Stitch lining to the foam between marks, stitching scant ½" (1.3 cm) from edges.

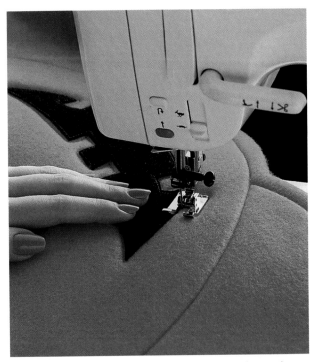

5) Trim foam close to stitching; trim remaining seam allowances to ¼" (6 mm). Turn the tabard right side out; press.

6) Fold in ½" (1.3 cm) seam allowances of opening; hand-stitch closed. Topstitch ½" (1.3 cm) from the outer edge of tabard. Stitch design lines as desired, avoiding belt loops.

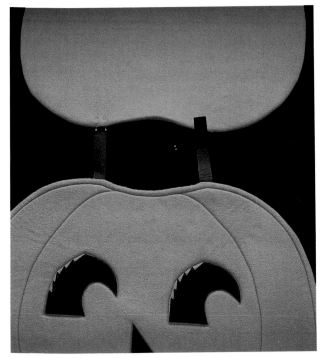

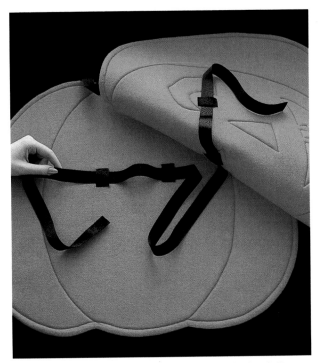

7) Repeat steps 4 and 5 for tabard back. Insert ends of shoulder straps at least ¾" (2 cm) into opening of tabard back at marks; pin. Check fit. Follow step 6, leaving straps pinned in place until they are caught in topstitching.

8) Attach any surface embellishments desired. Insert belt through belt loops.

Design-blocked Tabards

Often it is desirable to construct the tabard from two or more fabrics, sewn together in a pieced design. For example, a tabard for a bumble-bee costume would be made of pieced strips of black and yellow fabric. In the same way, a dragon tabard might have a breastplate of one fabric surrounded by another fabric for the main body. These effects are easily achieved, using a method called *design blocking*. Patterns are drawn for each block of the tabard design. The parts are first sewn together to make the front and back tabard panels. Then the tabard is completed following the instructions for a basic tabard.

✂ Cutting Directions

Cut one piece of the desired fabric for each of the design blocks in the pieced tabard panels, using the patterns as drawn opposite, steps 1 and 2. Cut interfacing, if desired.

Cut one tabard front and one tabard back from the lining. Cut one tabard front and one tabard back from the ¼" (6 mm) foam.

Cut two 6" (15 cm) pieces of ribbon for the shoulder straps. Cut four 4" (10 cm) pieces of ribbon for the belt loops. Cut a piece of ribbon for the belt, with the length equal to the waist measurement plus 20" (51 cm) for tying.

YOU WILL NEED

Paper, for drawing the pattern.

Fabric, for each component of the front and back panels, and for self-lining, if desired.

Interfacing, optional.

Lining fabric, for panels that are not self-lined.

¼" (6 mm) foam, for tabard interlining.

⅞" (2.2 cm) grosgrain ribbon, in color to match tabard or undergarment.

How to Draw a Pattern for a Design-blocked Tabard

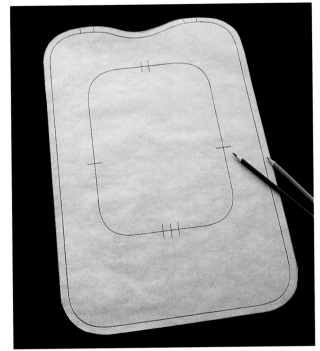

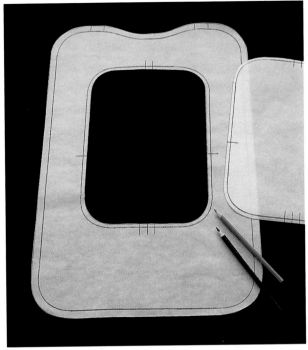

1) **Follow** the directions for drawing a pattern for a basic tabard on page 19, steps 1 and 2. Draw lines on pattern dividing it into desired design blocks. Mark matching guides across lines that divide blocks.

2) **Trace** each design block separately onto tracing paper; transfer matching guide marks. Add ¼" (6 mm) seam allowances along lines that do not already have seam allowances.

How to Sew a Design-blocked Tabard

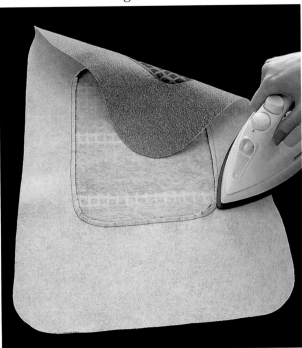

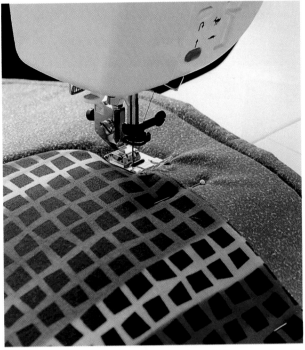

1) **Apply** interfacing, if desired, following manufacturer's directions. Staystitch and clip edges as necessary. Pin two adjoining blocks together, matching the guide marks. Stitch ¼" (6 mm) from edges. Press flat. Repeat for all blocks until entire tabard panel has been pieced together.

2) **Complete** tabard as on pages 20 and 21, steps 1 to 8. When stitching design lines in step 6, also stitch in the ditches of the seams between design blocks.

Legs, Tails & Stingers

Make a costume look more lifelike by adding a tail, extra legs, or even a stinger. Sew a long, thin tail with an optional contrasting tip or a thicker, padded tail with spikes, suitable for a dragon or dinosaur. Make jointed legs for insect costumes, with wire inserts, allowing them to be bent and shaped. Make a striped bee stinger to add impact to a bumble-bee tabard.

Tails and stingers can be sewn to the back of a tabard or full suit costume. To support the weight of a heavy tail on a tabard, a narrow, thin board, such as a ruler, can be inserted into a pocket sewn to the underside of the back panel.

Legs can be sewn into the seam at the outer edge of a tabard or into the side seams of a full suit costume. To help support the outer edge of a tabard with legs, heavy wire can be sewn around the outer edge, as on page 92, steps 3 and 4, before turning the tabard right side out.

Narrow tail with a contrasting tip (opposite) is suitable for many animal costumes. Jointed, bendable legs and a stinger, made from strip-pieced fabric, complete the bee tabard. Two layers of felt were fused together before the spikes for the dragon tail (above) were cut out.

✂ Cutting Directions

Cut a 5" (12.5 cm) strip of fabric and a 5" (12.5 cm) strip of foam for each leg, with the length equal to the desired finished length plus 1" (2.5 cm). Multiply the cut length of one strip by the number of legs plus one; cut a piece of cording with this length.

For a narrow tail, cut a 5" (12.5 cm) strip of fabric and a 5" (12.5 cm) strip of foam, with the length equal to the desired finished length of the tail plus 1" (2.5 cm).

For a narrow tail with a contrasting tip, cut a 5" (12.5 cm) strip of fabric, with the length equal to the desired finished length minus 1" (2.5 cm). Cut a 3" × 5" (7.5 × 12.5 cm) rectangle of contrasting plush felt or synthetic fur for the tip. Cut a 5" (12.5 cm) strip of foam interlining, with the length equal to the desired finished length of the tail plus 1" (2.5 cm). Cut a piece of cording, with the length equal to twice the finished length of the tail.

For a shaped tail or stinger, cut two pieces of fabric and two pieces of foam interlining, using the pattern as drawn on page 28, step 1. For a tail with spikes, cut one piece from felt or fused felt, using the pattern as drawn on page 28, step 2.

YOU WILL NEED

Fabric.

Plush felt or fur, for contrasting tip on narrow tail.

Felt or fused felt, for shaped tail with spikes.

1/4" (6 mm) foam, for interlining.

Silicone lubricant, for ease in sewing over foam, optional.

1/2" (1.3 cm) cording, for narrow tail or legs.

19-gauge wire, available at hardware stores, for legs or wired narrow tail.

Polyester fiberfill, for shaped tail or stinger.

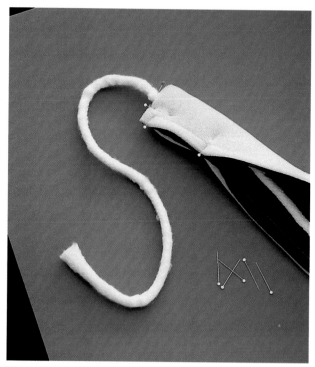

1) Pin foam strip to wrong side of fabric strip on long edges; baste within ½" (1.3 cm) seam allowance. Measure distance from one end of cording equal to cut length of leg minus 1½" (3.8 cm); mark.

2) Fold strip over cording, right sides together, placing one end of strip at mark on cording and extending fabric away from short end of cord. Pin long edges of fabric, matching raw edges.

3) Stitch ½" (1.3 cm) from long raw edges, taking care not to catch cording in stitches and stitching toward short end of cord. Pivot, and stitch across fabric strip, ½" (1.3 cm) from end of strip, centering cording.

4) Slide fabric onto short end of cord, turning fabric right side out and encasing cording inside strip. Cut off cording at stitched end. Color cut end of cording with permanent marker, if necessary.

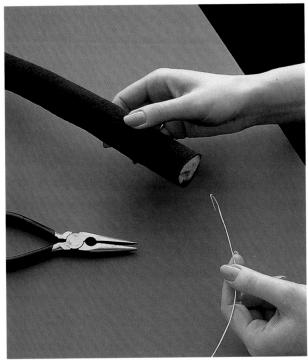

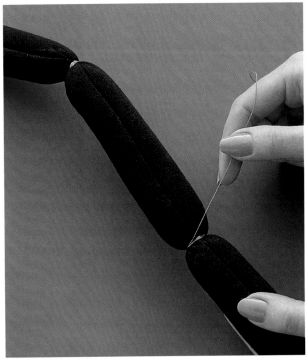

5) Repeat steps 1 to 4 for each leg. Discard excess cording. Cut wire to finished length of leg plus 1" (2.5 cm). Fold back ½" (1.3 cm) at ends of wire; insert into leg. Baste ⅜" (1 cm) from open end of leg. Attach legs to costume, catching end of leg in seam of costume.

6) Determine locations of joints, if desired. Wrap heavy thread several times around leg at joint; knot securely. Repeat for all joints.

How to Sew a Narrow Tail

1) Sew tail as in steps 1 to 4, opposite, for legs. Discard excess cording. Insert wire, if desired, as in step 5, above. Turn in open end of tail; hand-stitch tail to costume in desired location.

Tail with contrasting tip. Pin contrasting tip to one end of fabric strip for tail, right sides together. Stitch ½" (1.3 cm) seam; press open. Complete as in step 1, left.

How to Sew a Shaped Tail or Stinger

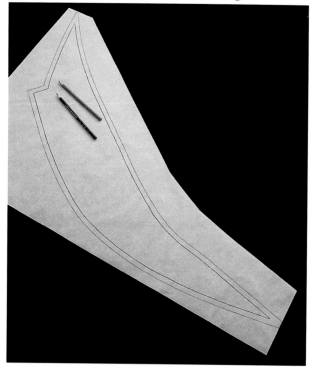

1) Determine desired finished size and shape of tail or stinger, including angle of attachment. Draw pattern for one side on paper; add ½" (1.3 cm) seam allowances around all edges.

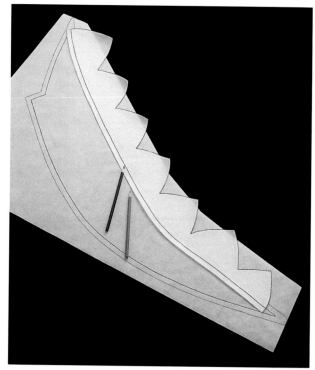

2) Draw pattern for spikes, if desired, tracing upper seamline of tail for lower edge of spikes; end spikes at least 1" (2.5 cm) from tail tip. Add ½" (1.3 cm) seam allowance to lower edge of spike pattern. Cut out pattern; cut out spikes.

3) Pin fabric, right side up, to foam; baste within ½" (1.3 cm) seam allowance. Repeat for second piece. For stinger or tail without spikes, omit step 4.

4) Pin spikes to one tail piece, right sides together, matching lower edge of spikes to upper edge of tail; clip spike seam allowance as necessary. Baste within ½" (1.3 cm) seam allowance.

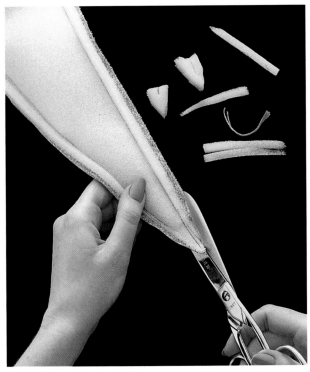

5) Pin tail or stinger pieces right sides together. Stitch around outer edges, leaving opening at end of attachment. Trim seam at tail tip; clip curves. Turn tail right side out.

6) Stuff tail or stinger lightly with polyester fiberfill, if desired. Turn in opening edges. Hand-stitch tail to back of costume in desired location.

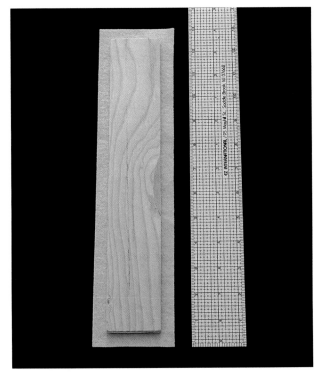

Tail support on tabard. 1) Cut thin wooden support to measure about 2" × 12" (5 × 30.5 cm), or use a wooden ruler. Cut felt pocket 1" (2.5 cm) larger than support.

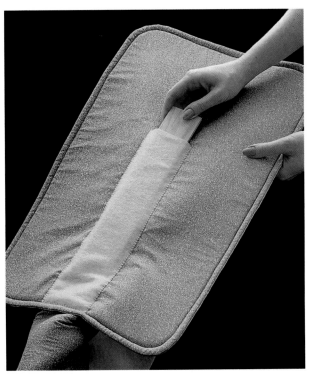

2) Pin pocket to underside of back panel of tabard, extending above and below the location of the tail attachment. Hand-stitch pocket to tabard along sides and lower edge. Slide support into pocket.

Raw-edge Appliqués

Raw-edge appliqués are an easy way to add patches of color or design features to costume parts, such as a tabard, gown, wings, or a hat. A paper-backed fusible web is used to affix the fabric shapes to the costume surface. For durability, a simple straight stitch is applied around the outer edges of the shapes.

How to Sew Raw-edge Appliqués

1) Draw or transfer the desired shapes onto paper backing of fusible web. For directional shapes, draw mirror images of desired finished shapes. Apply paper-backed fusible web to wrong side of appliqué fabrics, following manufacturer's directions.

2) Cut out shapes. Remove paper backing. Position shapes in desired locations on costume fabric, fusible side down. Fuse shapes, following manufacturer's directions.

3) Stitch around each shape, ⅛" (3 mm) from raw edges, using short to medium-length straight stitch.

Layered appliqués. Follow step 1 for all shapes of the design. Follow steps 2 and 3 for the first layer of shapes. Repeat steps 2 and 3 for each succeeding layer of shapes.

Gowns

Various Halloween costumes begin with a gown. A simple, loose-fitting gown can be sewn in any size desired, without using a pattern. The fabric is folded, marked, and cut according to the individual's body measurements.

Several sleeve styles can be used, depending on the look desired. You may select wide, sweeping sleeves for a wizard costume; full, gathered sleeves for an angel or princess costume; or long, narrow sleeves for a witch. The gown is cut as one piece, with the width of the fabric running from sleeve hem to sleeve hem. Follow the instructions below to determine the yardage needed.

Determining Yardage

Measure (a) from the shoulder to the desired finished length of the gown; add 1" (2.5 cm) for the hem allowance. Multiply this measurement by 2 to determine the cut length needed. Position arms down at the sides of the body; measure (b) from one wrist up the arm, across the back of the shoulders, and down the other arm to the wrist. Add 2" (5 cm) for sleeve hems. Allow at least 2" (5 cm) of extra length for gathered sleeves. If the fabric is wide enough to include the full sleeve length, purchase the fabric yardage determined in measurement (a), above. If the fabric is not wide enough to include the full sleeve length, purchase enough additional fabric to equal the desired circumference of the sleeve at the hem plus 1" (2.5 cm) for seam allowances.

✂ Cutting Directions

Cut the fabric with the length and width equal to the measurements determined above. If additional fabric is needed for the sleeve length, cut two sleeve extensions, with the length equal to the desired finished circumference of the sleeve hem plus 1" (2.5 cm), and the width equal to half of the total additional width needed plus 2" (5 cm) for hem and seam allowances.

YOU WILL NEED

Fabric; if possible, select fabric with width that equals or exceeds total arm length (above).

Single-fold bias tape, in color to match fabric.

⅜" (1 cm) elastic, for gown with gathered sleeves.

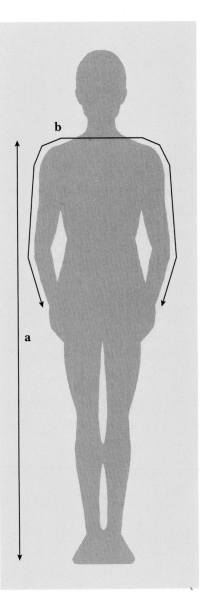

How to Sew a Simple Gown

1) Pin sleeve extensions, if needed, to sides of long fabric piece, right sides together, matching centers of pieces. Sew ½" (1.3 cm) seams. Press seams toward sleeve extensions. Fold entire fabric piece in half crosswise, right sides together, and again, lengthwise. Lay on flat surface.

2) Measure around the base of neck at the desired neckline placement; divide by 6.28. Draw an arc with a radius of this measurement from the folded center point. Cut on the marked line. Cut a 4" (10 cm) slit from neckline down center back. Cut slit deeper to accommodate wing harness (page 93), if necessary. Cut neck opening ½" (1.3 cm) deeper at front.

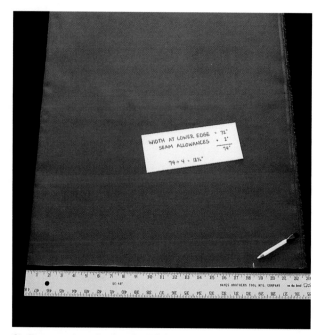

3) Determine desired width of lower edge plus 2" (5 cm) for seam allowances; divide by 4, and measure this distance from fold at lower edge; mark.

4) Measure the chest. Add 6" to 10" (15 to 25.5 cm) for ease and seam allowances; divide by 4. Lay a ruler parallel to the center fold, a distance from the fold equal to this measurement. Measure the back length from the base of the neck to the waist; multiply this measurement by .75. Mark point for the underarm along the ruler, a distance from upper fold equal to this measurement.

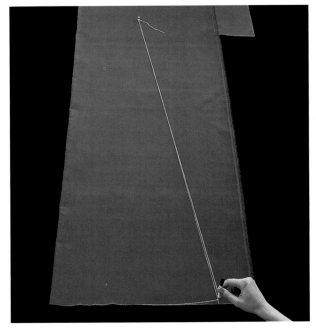

5) Draw side seamline from mark at lower edge to underarm point. Using string-and-pencil compass, curve lower edge of gown so that length of side seam equals length from underarm to lower edge, parallel to center fold.

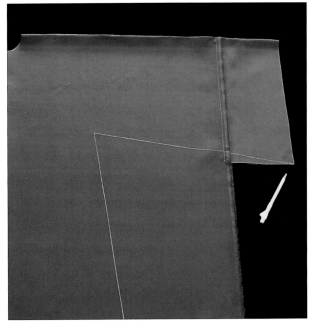

6) Draw line from underarm to lower corner of the sleeve extension. For gown without sleeve extensions, draw line to point on outer edge of fabric, a distance from upper fold equal to desired sleeve depth plus ½" (1.3 cm).

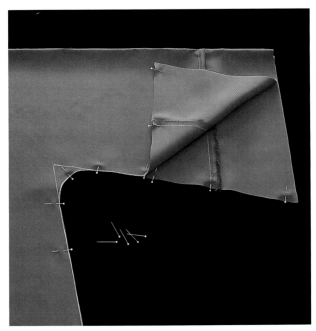

7) Round the underarm angle. Cut out gown on marked lines, cutting through all layers. Pin top two layers together from the lower edge of gown to the lower edge of sleeve. Repeat for bottom two layers. Unfold fabric.

8) Stitch side seam from lower edge of gown to lower edge of sleeve, stitching ½" (1.3 cm) from cut edges; repeat for opposite side. Clip underarm curves. Finish seams, if desired.

(Continued on next page)

9) Open out one folded edge of bias tape; align the edge of slit to the edge of tape, right sides up, with the end of tape at top of neckline. Set machine for short stitch length. Stitch scant ¼" (6 mm) seam, tapering inward to a point just below slit; stop with needle in fabric.

10) Continue stitching up opposite side of slit to the neckline. Cut the tape even with neckline.

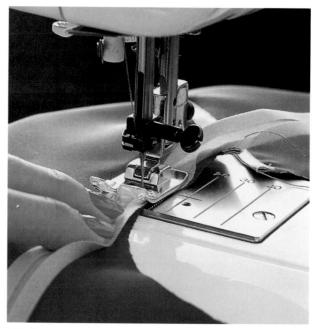

11) Wrap the tape around to right side of gown, just covering the stitching line with the fold of tape; pin. Edgestitch along fold from right side.

12) Open out one folded edge of bias tape; align edge of tape to neckline edge at one side of opening, right side of tape to wrong side of neckline, leaving 10" (25.5 cm) tail of tape for tying. Stitch along the foldline of tape to opposite side of neckline opening; cut tape, leaving 10" (25.5 cm) tail.

13) Fold tails in half, aligning the folded edges; pin. Wrap the remaining tape around to right side of the neckline, just covering the stitching line with the fold of tape; pin. Edgestitch along the fold from the right side, beginning at end of one tail, continuing around neckline, and ending at end of opposite tail.

14) Finish the lower edge of gown with overlock or zigzag stitch. Press under 1" (2.5 cm) for hem; stitch. Repeat for sleeve hems, for gowns that do not have gathered sleeves.

How to Sew a Gown with Gathered Sleeves

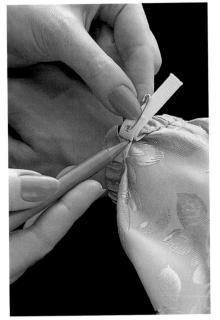

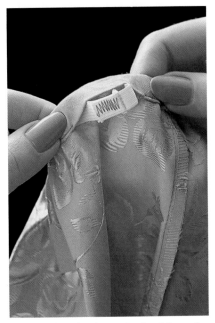

1) Sew the gown as on pages 34 to 37, steps 1 to 14. Press under ½" (1.3 cm) twice on lower edge of the sleeve. Stitch close to the first fold, leaving opening for inserting the elastic.

2) Cut elastic, with length equal to the wrist measurement plus 1" (2.5 cm). Thread elastic through the casing, using a safety pin or bodkin. Try on gown, and mark elastic for a comfortable fit around wrist.

3) Cut the elastic to desired length plus ½" (1.3 cm). Overlap ends of elastic ½" (1.3 cm). Stitch back and forth through both layers, using wide zigzag stitch or three-step zigzag stitch. Ease elastic back into casing. Stitch casing opening closed.

Full Suit Costumes

Full suit costumes can be made in any style desired, using a commercial pattern for a one-piece pajama or jumpsuit, or a two-piece sweat suit. The pattern may have a hood, or a separate padded hood (page 56) can be made. For infants and toddlers, the pattern may include feet. If the pattern does not have feet, the costume can be designed with separate spats (page 115), if desired, or an attached shoe flap can be added at the bottom of the leg front.

Design inserts can be sewn to the costume for added details, such as a furry back or a soft tummy patch. These inserts are made from fabric that does not ravel, such as felt or synthetic fur. To reduce bulk, the costume fabric is cut away from behind the insert.

✂ Cutting Directions

Prepare the pattern for a design insert, if desired, following step 1, below. Prepare the pattern for shoe flaps, if desired, as on page 40, steps 1 to 3. Cut out the costume pieces, using the prepared patterns.

YOU WILL NEED

Commercial pattern for one-piece pajama or jumpsuit, or two-piece sweat suit.

Tracing paper.

Nonraveling fabric, such as felt or synthetic fur, for design insert.

Lining for costume with shoe flaps.

¼" (6 mm) foam, for shoe flap interlining.

⅜" (1 cm) elastic, for costume with shoe flaps.

Notions as listed on pattern envelope.

How to Sew a Costume with a Design Insert

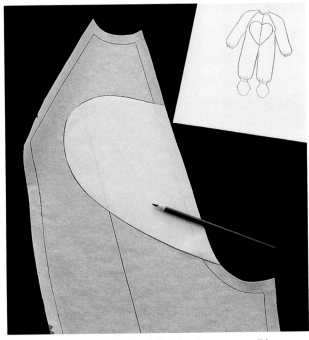

1) Draw sketch of desired finished costume. Place tracing paper over pattern in desired area for design insert. Draw outline of insert; cut out insert pattern. Mark placement of insert on costume pattern. Cut costume and inserts from fabric.

2) Place insert over costume piece in desired location; pin. Stitch close to outer edge of insert. Trim away costume fabric from behind insert. Complete costume, following pattern instructions.

How to Sew a Costume with Shoe Flaps

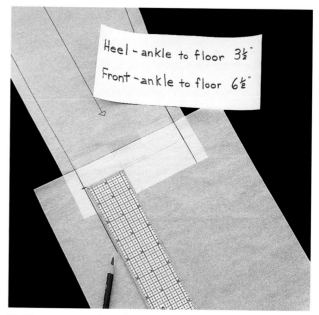

1) Measure heel from ankle to floor over shoe; measure front of foot from ankle to floor over toe of shoe. Record measurements. Mark leg hemline on back and front patterns. Draw a line 1" (2.5 cm) below hemline on back pattern for elastic casing; draw a line 1" (2.5 cm) above hemline on front pattern.

2) Tape rectangle of tracing paper over front pattern, using removable tape; align upper edge of paper to the line drawn in step 1. Extend the side seamlines a distance from hemline equal to heel measurement, as determined in step 1.

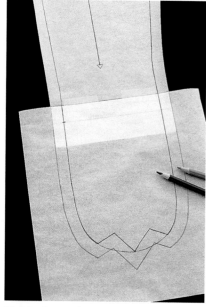

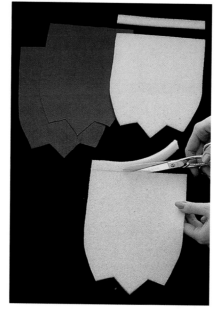

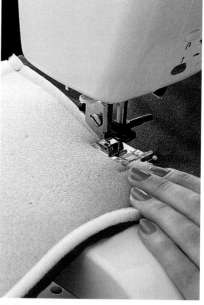

3) Mark a point at center front, a distance below hemline equal to front foot measurement plus 1" (2.5 cm). Draw curved line through marked point, connecting ends of side seamlines. Draw toes or claws along curve of shoe flap, if desired. Add ⅝" (1.5 cm) seam allowance along outer edge of shoe flap.

4) Cut out costume pieces. Remove the extension from front pattern piece; cut two pieces from lining and two from foam, using pattern extension. Trim ¾" (2 cm) from upper edges of foam pieces.

5) Baste foam to wrong side of extension, ⅜" (1 cm) from outer edge. Baste ¼" (6 mm) from upper edge of foam.

6) Press under ¼" (6 mm) at the lower edge of back leg; press under ¾" (2 cm) again, for casing. Open upper fold of casing. Pin front to back, right sides together. Stitch side and inseams, stopping at upper foldline of back leg casing.

7) Press under ¼" (6 mm) for the casing at upper edge of lining. Pin the lining to shoe flap, right sides together. Stitch outer edge of shoe flap, beginning and ending at the hemline. On one side, open folds and stitch lining casing to back casing; press seams open.

8) Trim the foam close to stitching. Trim seam allowance to ¼" (6 mm) along the curve. Clip corners. Turn right side out. Topstitch ¼" (6 mm) from outer edge of shoe flap.

9) Refold casing. Stitch upper edge of casing close to fold. Stitch lower edge of front casing ⅝" (1.5 cm) below first stitching line. Insert elastic through opening at seam; adjust for comfortable fit. Stitch securely.

10) Determine desired position and length for elastic strap to hold the shoe flap in place over shoe; mark. Stitch elastic to shoe flap. Complete costume, following pattern instructions.

Witch Hats

A witch's black hat, with a tall pointed crown and a wide, floppy brim, can set the mood for the rest of the costume. To give the hat more character, the pointed crown can be crumpled and bent. The edge of the brim is wired, allowing the wearer to shape it in dramatic curves.

✂ Cutting Directions

Cut one crown, one brim, and one brim lining from the fabric, following the pattern as drawn on page 46, steps 1 to 3. Cut one crown and one brim from interfacing.

YOU WILL NEED

1⅛ yd. (1.05 m) black fabric, at least 45" (115 cm) wide.

1⅛ yd. (1.05 m) mediumweight fusible interfacing.

Heavy-gauge milliner's wire, available in fabric stores, or 19-gauge wire, available at hardware stores.

Grosgrain ribbon, 1" (2.5 cm) wide, with length equal to circumference of head plus 2" (5 cm).

Heavy-gauge chenille stem.

Plastic spider; invisible thread.

How to Draw a Pattern for a Witch Hat

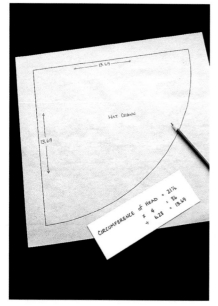

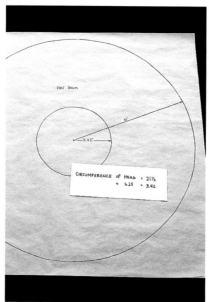

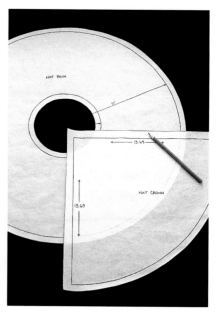

1) Measure the circumference of the head loosely, just above the ears. Multiply this measurement by 4 and divide the answer by 6.28. Draw a quarter circle with this radius, for the crown of the hat. Straight edges are center back of crown.

2) Divide the head circumference measurement by 6.28 to determine the radius of the inner brim. Draw a circle with this radius. Draw another circle from the same center point with a radius of 11" (28 cm).

3) Add ½" (1.3 cm) seam allowances to all curved edges. Add ¾" (2 cm) seam allowances to center back edges of the hat crown. Cut out patterns.

How to Sew a Witch Hat

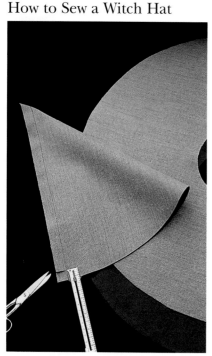

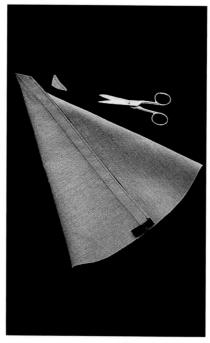

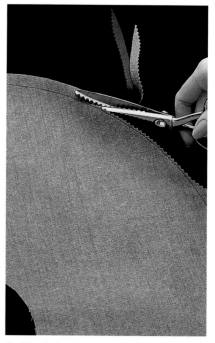

1) Fuse interfacing to crown and brim of hat. Stitch center back seam of crown, right sides together, stitching ¾" (2 cm) from raw edges. Clip seam allowances to stitching line, ⅝" (1.5 cm) above curved edge.

2) Stitch seam allowances together above clip, ⅛" (3 mm) from raw edges; press to one side. Trim seam allowances at point. Press seam allowances open below clip.

3) Pin brim lining to brim along outer curved edge; stitch ½" (1.3 cm) from edges. Trim seam close to stitching line, using pinking shears.

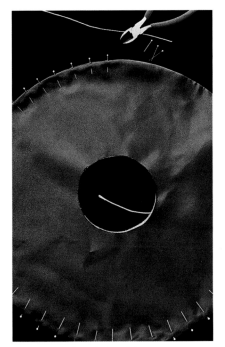

4) Turn brim right side out; press, centering seam along outer edge. Insert milliner's wire between brim and facing, snug against the outer seam; pin in place. Cut wire so ends overlap about 2" (5 cm).

5) Stitch ¼" (6 mm) from outer edge of brim, using zipper foot and encasing wire between stitching line and outer edge.

6) Stitch brim and facing together scant ½" (1.3 cm) from inner curved edge. Clip seam allowance close to stitching line every ½" (1.3 cm).

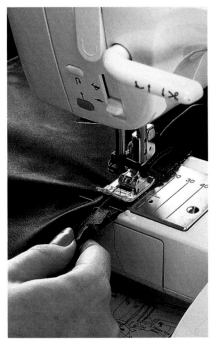

7) Pin brim to crown, right sides together, matching raw edges; stitch ½" (1.3 cm) seam.

8) Pin grosgrain ribbon to seam allowance, aligning edge of ribbon to seamline; turn under upper end, and overlap ends of ribbon at back of hat. Stitch along edge of ribbon. Turn seam allowance and ribbon into crown; press.

9) Insert chenille stem into space between stitching lines on crown seam. Crumple crown as desired. Tie invisible thread around spider and secure to edge of brim, if desired.

Medieval Hats

Any girl would love to own a medieval lady-in-waiting hat, whether for a Halloween costume party or just for dressing up and having fun.

This style features a long, sheer veil that flows from the top of a tall crown. The brim is made from jumbo cording covered with shimmery gathered fabric for a luxurious look.

The same hat, without the veil, could be used for a wizard costume. For additional embellishment, celestial shapes can be appliquéd to the crown.

✄ Cutting Directions

Cut one crown from the fabric, using the pattern as drawn below. Cut a strip of fabric 6" (15 cm) wide from the full width of the crosswise grain of the fabric, for the brim. Cut a piece of jumbo cording, with the length equal to the circumference of the head plus 8" (20.5 cm). Cut one crown from the interfacing.

YOU WILL NEED

¾ yd. (0.7 m) mediumweight fabric, at least 45" (115 cm) wide, for crown and brim.

⅝ yd. (0.6 m) mediumweight fusible interfacing.

1½ yd. (1.4 m) lightweight sheer fabric, up to 45" (115 cm) wide, for veil.

Grosgrain ribbon, 1" (2.5 cm) wide, with length equal to circumference of head plus 2" (5 cm), for hat without veil.

1 yd. (0.95 m) narrow ribbon, for ties.

Jumbo cording.

Lightweight cord, such as pearl cotton.

Wooden dowel, ¼" (6 mm) in diameter.

How to Sew a Medieval Hat

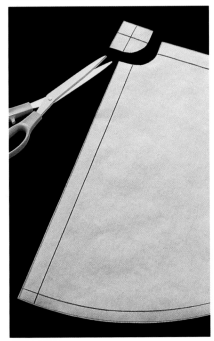

1) Draw a pattern, following steps 1 and 3 at the top of page 46. For hat with veil, draw an arc with radius of 1" (2.5 cm) from point of crown; trim away. For hat without veil, construct crown as on page 46, steps 1 and 2; then continue, beginning with step 6 on page 50.

2) Fuse interfacing to crown of hat. Staystitch ½" (1.3 cm) from upper and lower curves, sewing with short stitches. Clip upper seam allowance to stitching line every ¼" (6 mm).

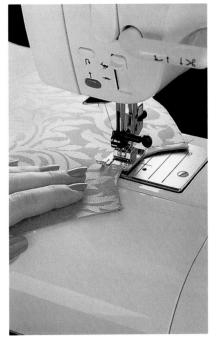

3) Turn down the upper seam allowance, rolling stitching line to wrong side; press. Stitch ¼" (6 mm) from pressed edge, securing seam allowance to crown.

(Continued on next page)

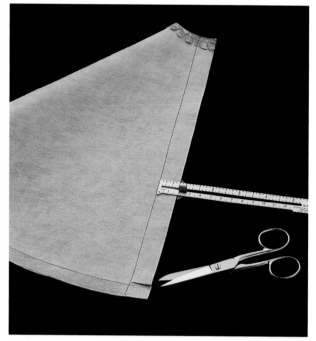

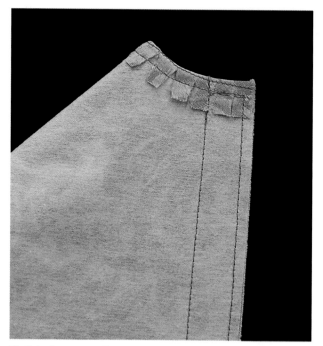

4) Stitch center back seam of crown, right sides together, stitching ¾" (2 cm) from raw edges. Clip seam allowances to stitching line, ⅝" (1.5 cm) above lower curved edge.

5) Stitch seam allowances together above clip to upper edge, ⅛" (3 mm) from raw edges. Pivot, and stitch to seamline, ¼" (6 mm) from top; backstitch to secure. Press seam allowance to one side. Press seam allowances open below clip.

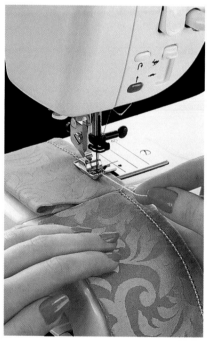

6) Stitch brim strip together into a continuous circle, leaving 3" (7.5 cm) opening at center of seam; press seam allowance open. Divide circle into fourths; mark.

7) Fold circle, wrong sides together, matching raw edges. Zigzag over a cord, stitching ⅜" (1 cm) from the raw edges.

8) Divide lower edge of crown into fourths; mark. Pin brim to crown, right sides together, matching marks; pull up cord to distribute gathers evenly. Stitch ½" (1.3 cm) from raw edge. For hat without veil, follow step 8 on page 47, then steps 12 and 13, opposite.

9) Finish one cut edge of veil, using overlock or narrow hem. Run two rows of gathering stitches within ½" (1.3 cm) seam allowance on opposite cut edge; divide edge into fourths, and mark.

10) Pin ribbon ties at side marks, if desired. Pin veil to lower edge of hat, matching marks; align selvages of veil to back seamline of crown. Pull up on threads to distribute gathers evenly. Stitch ½" (1.3 cm) from raw edges. Trim seam allowances of veil and brim.

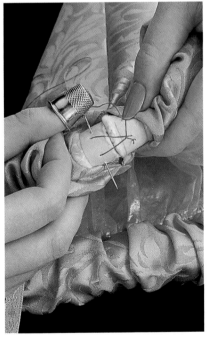

11) Turn veil, seam allowances, and ribbon into crown. Pull veil through inside of hat and out hole at top of crown. Edgestitch through crown, seam allowances, and veil, just above the brim, keeping back crown seam allowances free.

12) Cut dowel ¾" (2 cm) shorter than length of center back seam; insert dowel into space between stitching lines on crown seam. Tack opening closed.

13) Wrap ends of jumbo cording with tape. Insert cording through opening in brim; butt ends, and hand-stitch together through tape. Hand-stitch opening closed.

Crowns & Halos

A gleaming crown is important for any royal costume. This style crown is sewn from metallic fabric, padded with thin foam. Sew-on or glue-on gemstones provide a glitzy finishing touch.

A sparkling halo is the perfect topper for an adorable angel or fairy. A metallic fabric tube is stuffed with cording for a soft halo that rests on top of the head. Wired metallic garland or bead trim can be wrapped around the halo, and shimmering streamers of ribbons, beads, or decorative cords can be attached at the back.

✂ Cutting Directions

For the crown, cut two rectangles from fabric, one from interfacing, and one from foam, cutting the rectangles larger than the crown pattern.

For a plain halo, cut one rectangle of fabric, with the length equal to the measurement around the head plus 1" (2.5 cm) and the width equal to the circumference of the cording plus 1" (2.5 cm) for seam allowances.

For a gathered halo, cut one rectangle of fabric, with the length equal to two times the measurement around the head plus 1" (2.5 cm) and the width equal to the circumference of the cording plus 1" (2.5 cm) for seam allowances.

YOU WILL NEED

Crown:

Tricot-backed metallic fabric.

Lightweight fusible interfacing.

Foam, ¼" (6 mm) thick.

Sew-on or glue-on gemstones.

Halo:

Tricot-backed metallic fabric.

Cording, ½" (1.3 cm) in diameter.

Decorative trims, such as wired metallic garland, beads, ribbons, and decorative cords.

Additional embellishments as desired.

How to Sew a Crown

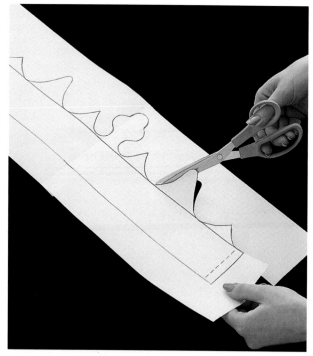

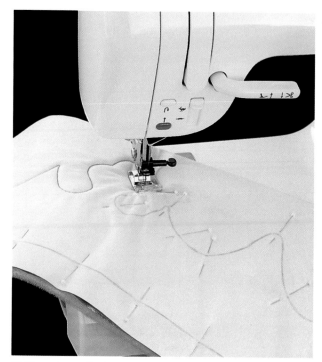

1) Draw rectangle on paper 2½" (6.5 cm) wide, with length equal to circumference of the head plus 2" (5 cm). Draw the desired design above upper long edge of rectangle, beginning and ending design no less than ½" (1.3 cm) from ends of rectangle. Cut out pattern.

2) Fuse interfacing to wrong side of one fabric rectangle. Transfer crown pattern outline to wrong side of remaining rectangle. Layer fabric, right sides together, over rectangle of foam, with pattern outline on top. Stitch along top line of pattern outline; stitch along bottom line to within 4" (10 cm) of ends.

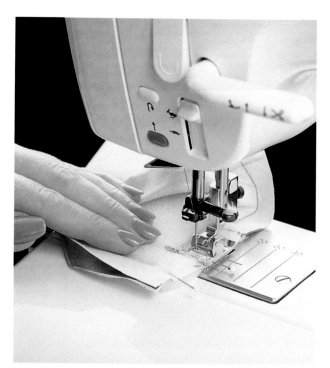

3) Trim fabric and foam close to stitching. Cut all layers on marked lines at ends. At unstitched sections of lower line, trim fabric to ½" (1.3 cm); trim foam even with line. Clip curves; trim corners.

4) Turn right side out. Stitch the ends together ½" (1.3 cm) from the edges, matching seams. Trim the fabric and foam close to stitching. Fold under ½" (1.3 cm) at opening; hand-stitch closed. Stitch or glue gemstones to crown, if desired.

How to Sew a Halo

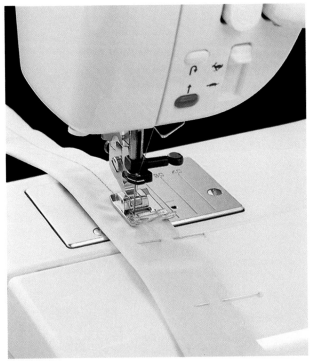

1) Fold rectangle of halo fabric in half lengthwise; pin. Stitch ½" (1.3 cm) from long raw edge; if stitching on stretchy knit fabric, use narrow zigzag stitch. Turn tube right side out.

2) Wrap cording around forehead; wrap cording with tape at overlap. Mark line on tape at overlap; cut on marked line through tape. Insert cording through fabric tube, using a safety pin.

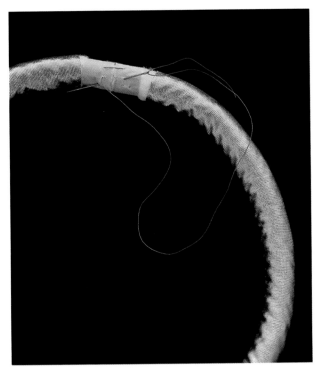

3) Butt the ends of cording; hand-stitch together, stitching through tape. Smooth fabric tube over joined ends; turn under ½" (1.3 cm) on one end of fabric tube, and lap over remaining end. Slipstitch ends of fabric tube together. For gathered halo, distribute gathers evenly.

4) Wrap halo with decorative trims. Cut several lengths of ribbons and trims, 1 yd. (0.95 m) long. Stitch trims together securely at center; hand-stitch to back of halo. Add other embellishments as desired.

Padded Hoods

Create an impressive head for your costume with a padded hood. Foam, sewn between the outer layer and lining, helps support the hood and any other items attached to it. Since it does not cover the face, a padded hood allows for a full range of vision.

A variety of hood ornaments can be made and attached to the padded hood. Lion manes and features such as ears, horns, eyes, and antennae can be made and attached after completion of the basic hood. Wired flower petals can be made and sewn around the face opening during construction. Features such as dragon spikes can be sewn into the center top and back seam during construction.

Patterns for two hood styles are given on page 63. The loose-fitting hood can be used for a slightly oversized, larger-than-life appearance. This is especially effective for animal costumes. For some costumes, such as the zinnia, it is more desirable to have a hood that fits the head more snugly. The closer fit helps support the flower petals around the face.

✄ Cutting Directions

Draw the pattern for the hood as on page 58, step 1. Measure over the head to the desired length for the hood; divide this measurement by two, and add 1" (2.5 cm) for seam allowances. Adjust the pattern length, if necessary. Cut two pieces from the fabric, two pieces from the lining, and two pieces from the foam interlining. Cut a rectangle of fabric, 2" × 4" (5 × 10 cm), for the closure underlap.

For a hood with petals, draw a pattern as on page 82, planning nine petals to fit around the hood opening, between marked dots, plus one petal that will be attached under the chin. Cut twenty pieces from the fabric; cut ten pieces from the foam.

YOU WILL NEED

Fabric, for hood.

Matching or contrasting fabric, for lining.

Foam, ¼" (6 mm) thick, for interlining.

Hook and loop tape.

Drawstring cording.

Materials for ears, horns, eyes, or antennae as on page 65, if desired.

Macramé cording; 10" (25.5 cm) cardboard template, for hood with lion mane.

Felt, for hood with dragon spikes.

Fabric; foam, ¼" (6 mm) thick; 19-gauge wire or heavy-gauge milliner's wire, for hood with petals.

Silicone lubricant, for ease in sewing over foam, optional.

How to Sew a Padded Hood

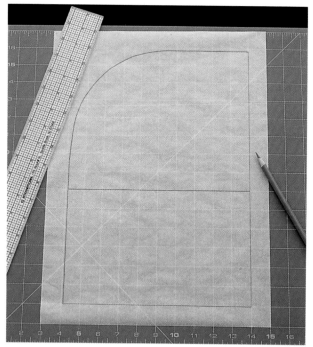

1) Place the tracing paper over a 1" (2.5 cm) grid. Draw full-size pattern for hood, using the half-size pattern on page 63 as a guide. Cut fabric, lining, and foam pieces. Transfer mark for end of casing to hood.

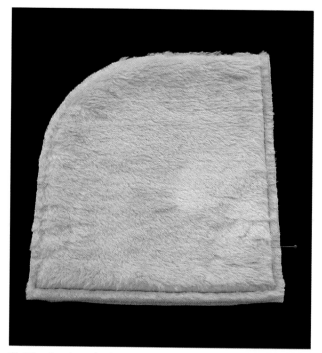

2) Pin the hood piece, right side up, to the foam piece; baste ⅜" (1 cm) from raw edges. Repeat for the remaining piece.

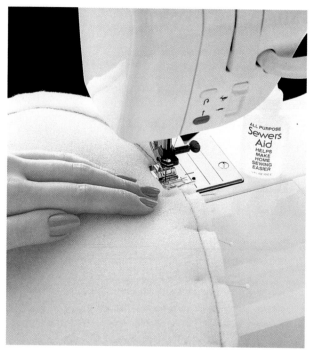

3) Stitch hood pieces, right sides together, along top and center back, stitching ½" (1.3 cm) from raw edges. Trim seam allowances to ¼" (6 mm). Apply silicone lubricant under presser foot and on bed of machine, if desired, to help foam feed evenly.

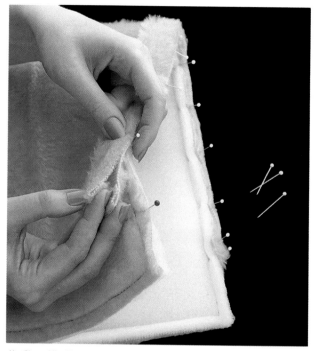

4) Cut 2" (5 cm) strip of fabric for casing, with length equal to the front opening between marks plus 1" (2.5 cm). Fold under ½" (1.3 cm) on ends of casing strip; fold strip in half lengthwise. Pin strip around front opening of hood between marks. Baste casing to hood ⅜" (1 cm) from raw edges.

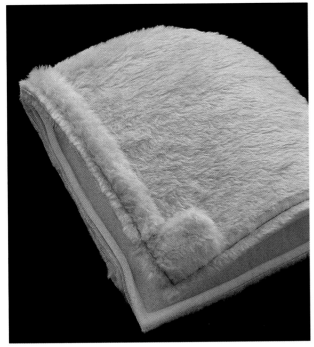

5) Fold closure underlap piece in half crosswise; stitch ¼" (6 mm) seams along edges perpendicular to fold. Turn right side out; press. Pin to left side of hood, right sides together, just under casing. Baste ⅜" (1 cm) from raw edges.

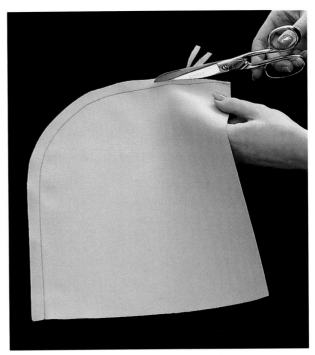

6) Stitch hood lining pieces, right sides together, along the top and center back seam, stitching ½" (1.3 cm) from raw edges. Trim seam allowances to ¼" (6 mm).

7) Pin hood to lining, right sides together, around front and bottom edges. Stitch ½" (1.3 cm) from raw edges, leaving an opening at bottom for turning. Trim seam allowances; clip corners. Turn right side out; press lightly. Slipstitch opening closed. Topstitch along lower edge.

8) Cut two pieces of hook and loop tape to length of closure underlap. Stitch loop tape to right side of underlap. Stitch hook tape to lining side of hood at corresponding location. Thread drawstring cording through casing, using a bodkin or safety pin. Make and attach head features (page 60 and pages 67 to 69) as desired.

How to Make a Hood with a Lion Mane

1) Cut macramé cording to the desired length for mane base plus 1" (2.5 cm); wrap tape around both ends. Wrap additional macramé cording around cardboard template. Cut wrapped cording at both ends to make 10" (25.5 cm) strands.

2) Center several strands over base, beginning ½" (1.3 cm) from end; pack the strands together densely. Stitch strands to base, using closely spaced, three-step zigzag stitch.

3) Continue stitching strands to base until entire base is covered. Pin mane to hood at placement line. Stitch the mane to the hood, using straight stitch and stitching over the previous stitches. Ravel strands of cording.

How to Make a Hood with Dragon Spikes

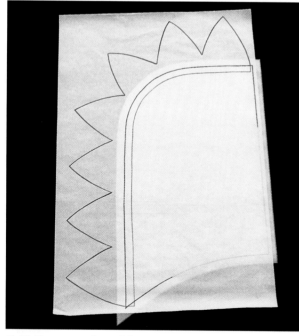

1) Follow steps 1 and 2 on page 58. Draw pattern for spikes, tracing curved seamline of hood for lower edge of spikes; begin and end spikes ⅛" (3 mm) from ends of seamline. Cut out spikes.

2) Pin the spikes to the curved edge of the hood, right sides together; clip spike seam allowance as necessary. Baste spikes to hood, within ½" (1.3 cm) seam allowance. Complete the hood as on pages 58 and 59, steps 3 to 8.

How to Make a Hood with Petals

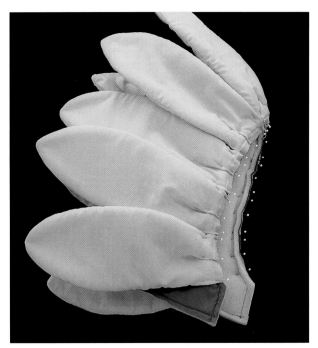

1) Make padded petals, following cutting directions on page 82 and step 2 on page 83. Set the machine for zigzag stitch with medium width and short length. Place wire just outside previous stitching, allowing the ends of wire to extend above upper cut edge. Stitch over wire around outer edge, beginning and ending ⅝" (1.5 cm) from upper cut edge. Trim wire even with cut edge; turn under ends of wire.

2) Follow steps 3 and 4 on page 83. Make hood as on page 58, steps 1 to 3. Pin nine petals to right side of hood, around the face opening, with bottom petals ¼" (6 mm) from marks for ends of casing; baste.

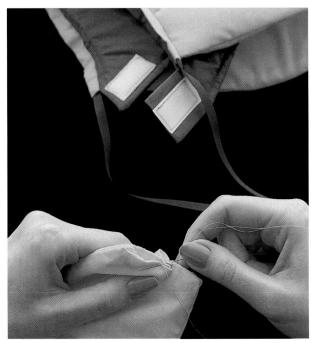

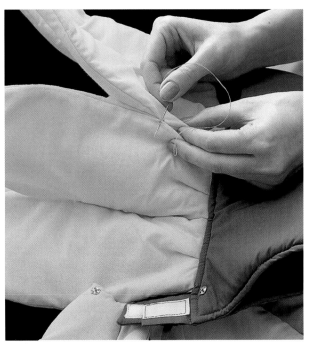

3) Complete hood, following steps 4 to 8 on pages 58 and 59. Topstitch ¼" (6 mm) from casing seam. Turn in ends of opening on the remaining petal ½" (1.3 cm), making ½" (1.3 cm) tuck in center; pin. Hand-stitch opening closed.

4) Tack the corner of petal to hood at side of closure; sew snap to opposite corner of petal and corresponding location on hood. Tack the other petals together 2" (5 cm) from face opening. Bend wires to hold petals out from face.

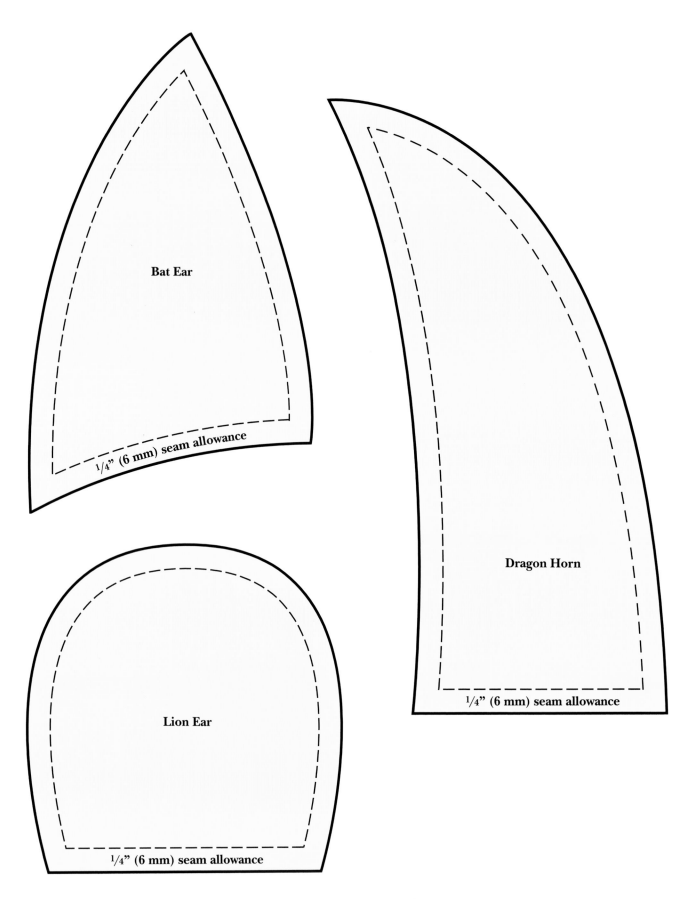

Bat Ear

¹/₄" (6 mm) seam allowance

Dragon Horn

¹/₄" (6 mm) seam allowance

Lion Ear

¹/₄" (6 mm) seam allowance

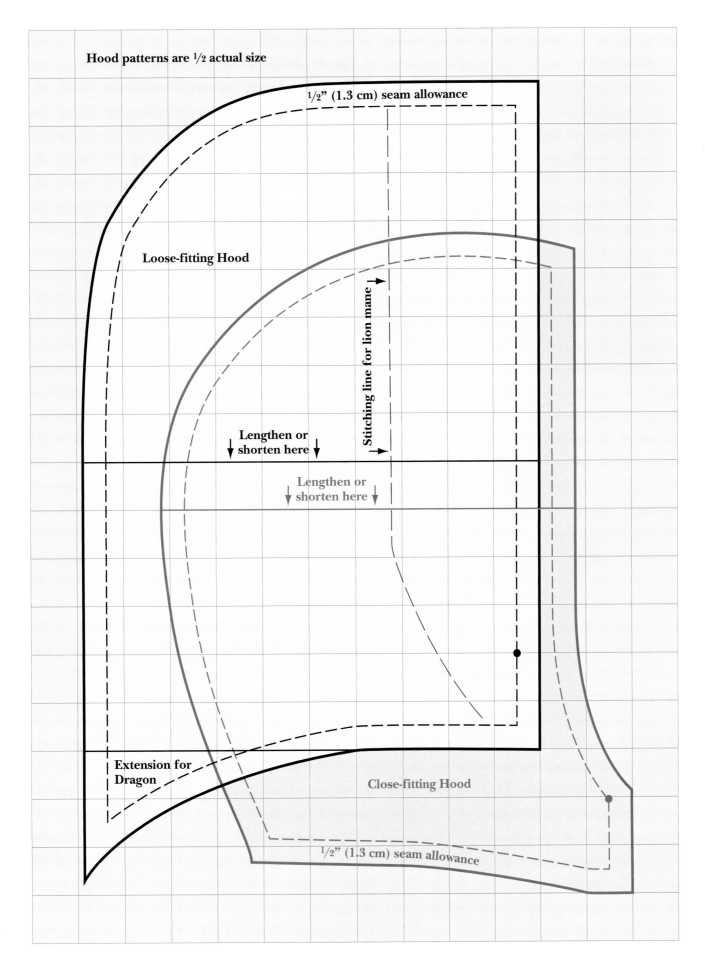

Hood patterns are ¹/₂ actual size

¹/₂" (1.3 cm) seam allowance

Loose-fitting Hood

Stitching line for lion mane

Lengthen or
shorten here

Lengthen or
shorten here

Extension for
Dragon

Close-fitting Hood

¹/₂" (1.3 cm) seam allowance

Simple Headgear

Make simple headgear from a purchased headband or ball cap. Cover the headband with fabric, and attach ears, horns, or antennae. Use basic ball caps to top off an animal, bird, or insect costume. Remove the bill from the cap, or leave the bill attached to represent the nose or beak, covering it with felt. For stiffness, fuse two layers of felt together before cutting. Attach ears, horns, eyes, or antennae to either style.

Patterns for horns and two ear styles are provided on page 62. Large glossy eyes can be made from two-piece plastic ball ornaments. Wire notebook springs or large chenille stems work well for antennae. For added whimsy and to cover sharp points, Styrofoam® balls or table tennis balls can be attached to the ends.

YOU WILL NEED

Headband; fabric for covering headband.

Fabric, for horns or ears.

Ball cap, in desired color; felt or fused felt, for cap with nose or beak.

Fabric; foam, ¼" (6 mm) thick; lining, interfacing, optional, for ears.

Fabric; foam, ¼" (6 mm) thick; polyester fiberfill, for horns.

Two-piece plastic ball ornament; spray adhesive and glitter, or craft acrylic paint; paper clip; pliers; heat source; fused fabric; glue, for eyes.

Two jumbo chenille stems, or one wire notebook spring; two small Styrofoam balls or table tennis balls; paint; hot glue, for antennae.

How to Cover a Headband with Fabric

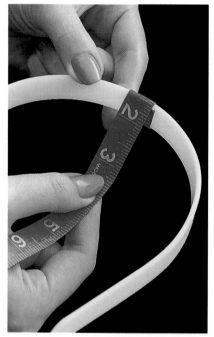

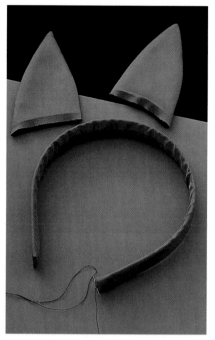

1) Measure circumference at widest point of the headband; cut strip of fabric, with width equal to the determined measurement plus ½" (1.3 cm) and length equal to length of headband plus ½" (1.3 cm).

2) Fold strip in half lengthwise; stitch ¼" (6 mm) from long raw edges. Center seam on one side of tube; stitch ¼" (6 mm) seam across one end. Clip corners. Turn right side out.

3) Insert headband into tube. Turn in ¼" (6 mm) on the open end of tube. Hand-stitch opening closed. Attach ears, horns, or antennae to headband as desired.

How to Make a Headpiece from a Ball Cap

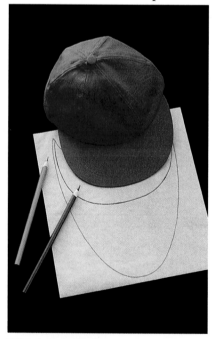

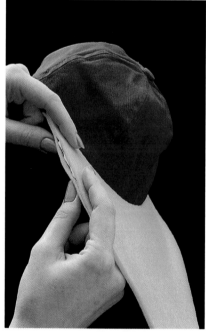

With brim. 1) Trace outer edge of brim on paper. Draw pattern for nose or beak, extending side edges slightly and curving front edge of brim as desired.

2) Cut two brim extensions from felt; glue extensions to the top and underside of brim, gluing extensions together beyond outer edge of brim. Attach ears, horns, eyes, or antennae as desired.

Without brim. 1) Remove stitches securing brim to cap; remove brim. Restitch the facing to the front of cap. Attach ears, horns, eyes, or antennae as desired.

How to Sew Ears

1) Trace desired pattern from page 62. Cut two pieces from fabric, two from lining, and two from interfacing, if desired; cut two pieces from foam for padded ears. Apply interfacing to the wrong side of ear pieces, if desired, following manufacturer's directions.

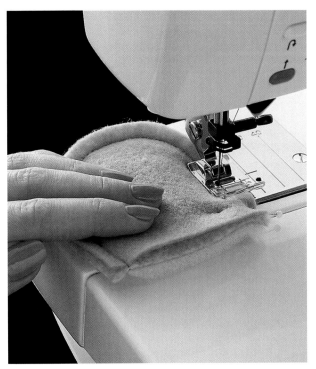

2) Pin ear and lining right sides together; for padded ear, layer ear pieces over foam. Stitch ¼" (6 mm) from raw edges, leaving opening along straight edge. Trim foam from seam allowance and ¼" (6 mm) from opening edge.

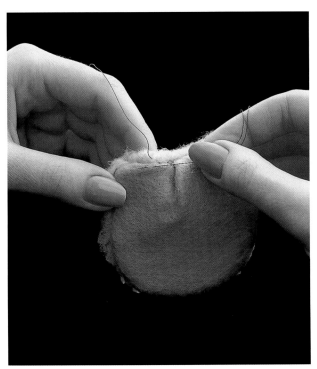

3) Turn right side out; press lightly. Turn in ¼" (6 mm) on bottom of ear. Hand-stitch or machine-stitch opening closed, making a small tuck at center of ear, if desired.

4) Hand-stitch ear to headband, ball cap, or hood at desired location.

How to Sew Horns

1) Trace pattern from page 62. Cut four pieces from fabric and four pieces from foam. Pin fabric, right side up, to foam; baste scant ¼" (6 mm) from raw edges.

2) Pin two horn pieces right sides together. Stitch ¼" (6 mm) from side edges. Trim seam at point; trim foam from opening edge. Turn horn right side out. Repeat for remaining pieces.

3) Stuff the horns with polyester fiberfill, if desired. Turn under ¼" (6 mm) around bottom of horns. Hand-stitch horns to headband, ball cap, or hood at the desired location.

How to Make Large Glossy Eyes

1) Spray inside of plastic ball halves with *light* coat of spray adhesive; sprinkle with glitter. Or paint the inside of the plastic ball halves as desired; allow to dry. Trim plastic hanger from ball, using mat knife or wire cutter.

2) Straighten one fold of paper clip. Grasp paper clip with pliers; heat end of wire over flame until metal is discolored. Insert end of wire into plastic ball about ⅛" (3 mm) from edge. Reheat paper clip and repeat two or three times, spacing holes evenly around edge of ball.

3) Hand-stitch eye to costume at holes. Cut strips of fused fabric to desired length and width for the eyelids. Cut slashes along one side to make eyelashes, if desired; curl lashes with pencil. Secure eyelids to edge of eye, using glue.

How to Make Antennae

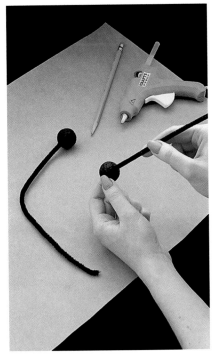

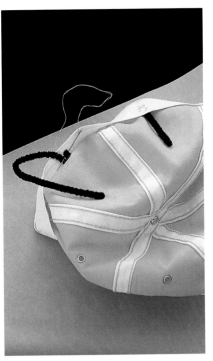

1) Make indentation in Styrofoam® balls, using pencil, or poke small hole in table tennis balls, using awl. Paint the balls as desired. Insert chenille stems or notebook springs into balls; secure with hot glue.

Securing chenille stems to cap or hood. Poke the stem through cap or hood to wrong side. Bend stem at desired length; turn under ¼" (6 mm) at end of stem. Hand-stitch to inside of cap or hood.

Securing chenille stems to the headband. Wrap end of the stem around the headband; twist around base of antenna at top of headband to secure.

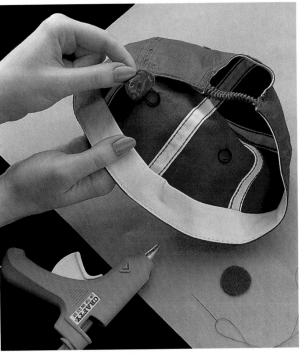

Securing springs to cap or hood. 1) Cut springs slightly longer than desired finished length, using wire cutter. Poke springs through cap or hood to wrong side. Rotate spring until two turns of spring are inside headgear; compress end of spring.

2) Cut two 1" (2.5 cm) felt circles. Secure circles over ends of springs, using generous amount of hot glue; allow to cool. Hand-stitch circles to the inside of cap or hood.

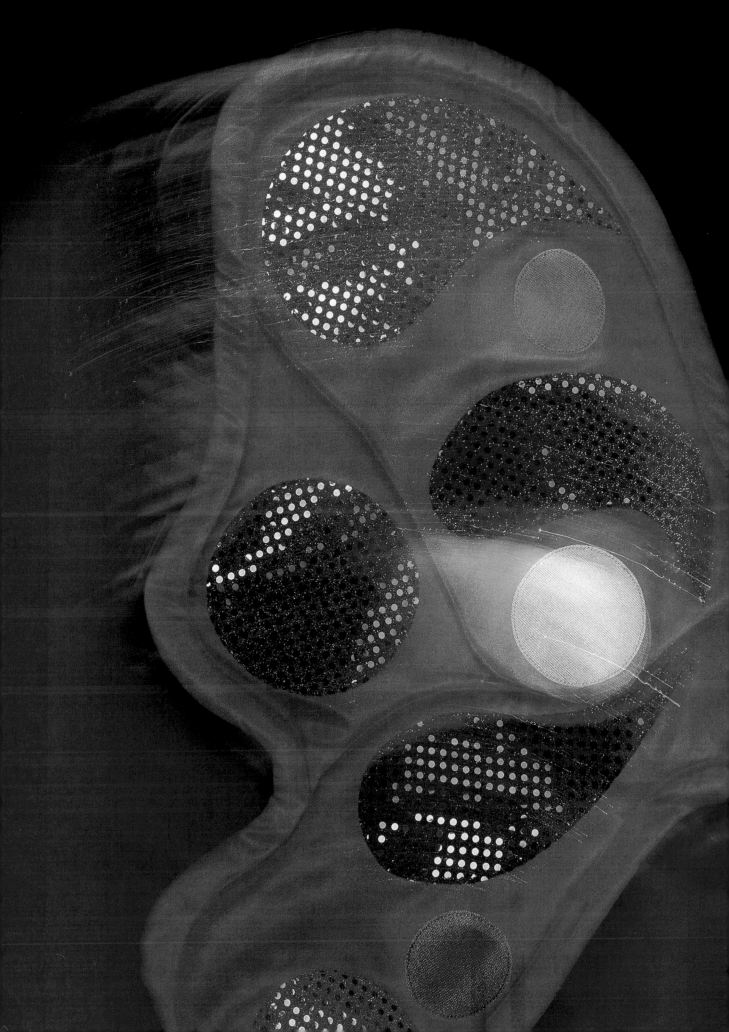

Capes, Skirts & Wings

Capes

A cape is a theatrical and very versatile costume element. Distinguished royalty, wizards and magicians, and even witches can benefit from the use of a cape.

In its simplest form, a cape is a circle of fabric, cut out and tied at the neck, and open down the front. An impressive lined cape can be made, using any stable fabrics for the outer surface and the contrasting lining. When cost and time are factors, an inexpensive cape can be made with minimal sewing, using felt. Either cape style can be made with or without a collar, and both are secured at the neck with ribbon ties.

The length of either cape style can be varied, depending on the desired look; fabric can be pieced to acquire a circle with the necessary diameter. However, to avoid piecing the felt, the circle diameter must be equal to or less than 72" (183 cm).

Felt cape without a collar (above) is a quick and easy way to make a cape fit for a king. The magician's cape (opposite) is fully lined and sports a stand-up collar for a more elaborate effect.

✄ Cutting Directions

For a lined cape, cut a square of fabric from the outer cape fabric and the lining fabric twice the desired length of the cape plus about 4" (10 cm). Piece two fabric widths together, if necessary. For the collar, cut one rectangle from the outer cape fabric and one from the lining, as on page 74, step 4.

For a felt cape, cut a square of fabric from felt twice the desired length of the cape plus about 3" (7.5 cm). For the collar, cut one rectangle from felt as on page 76, step 1.

YOU WILL NEED

Lined cape:

Fabric for cape and lining, amount depending on length of cape.

1 yd. (0.95 m) ribbon, for ties.

Interfacing, for collar.

Felt cape:

Felt, amount depending on length of cape.

Single-fold bias tape.

1 yd. (0.95 m) ribbon, for ties.

How to Sew a Lined Cape

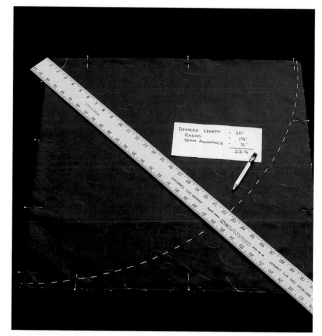

Cape with a collar. 1) Fold square of fabric for cape in half lengthwise, then crosswise. Pin layers together. Measure around base of neck. Divide measurement by 3.14; then divide result by 2 to find the radius. Mark an arc on fabric, for neck opening, measuring from folded center of fabric a distance equal to radius, using straightedge and pencil.

2) Mark an arc for lower edge of cape, measuring from folded center of fabric a distance equal to the desired length of cape plus measurement of radius determined in step 1, plus ½" (1.3 cm) for seam allowance at lower edge.

3) Cut on marked lines through all layers. Cut along one folded edge: this will be center front opening of cape. Cut lining, using outer cape as a pattern.

4) Measure the distance around the neck edge of cape from center front to center front, ½" (1.3 cm) from the neck edge. Cut rectangle for the collar from outer fabric and lining, measuring this length by desired width; collar width, not including ½" (1.3 cm) seam allowances, can range from 2½" to 4" (6.5 to 10 cm).

74

5) Cut and apply interfacing to wrong side of collar outer fabric, following manufacturer's directions. Pin the collar to lining, right sides together. Stitch ½" (1.3 cm) from raw edges, leaving one long edge open. Trim seam allowances; trim corners. Turn the collar right side out; press. Baste ⅜" (1 cm) from raw edges.

6) Staystitch around neck edge of outer cape fabric, ⅜" (1 cm) from raw edges; repeat for lining. Clip neck edges of outer cape and lining to staystitching. Pin-mark center of collar along raw edges and center back neck edge of cape and lining.

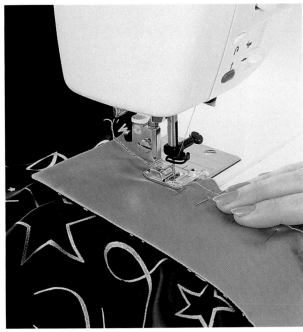

7) Pin the collar to right side of outer cape along the neck edge, positioning ends of the collar ½" (1.3 cm) from center front edge of the cape and matching pin marks. Stitch collar to cape a scant ½" (1.3 cm) from raw edges.

8) Pin outer cape to the lining, right sides together. Stitch ½" (1.3 cm) from the raw edges, leaving an opening along the neck edge for turning. Trim the corners. Turn the cape right side out; press. Turn under lining neck edge along the opening; stitch opening closed.

(Continued on next page)

How to Sew a Lined Cape (continued)

9) Cut ribbon for ties to desired length. Turn under ½" (1.3 cm) at one end of each tie; pin ribbon ties to center front at neck edge. Topstitch securely.

Cape without a collar. Follow page 74, steps 1 to 3. Continue as in step 6, omitting reference to collar. Follow step 8, turning under both raw edges of opening. Attach ties as in step 9.

How to Sew a Felt Cape

Cape with a collar. 1) Follow page 74, steps 1 to 3, omitting references to lining and seam allowances. Continue as in steps 4 and 6. Pin collar to cape along neck edge, right sides up, positioning ends of collar even with center front edges and matching pin marks. Stitch collar to cape, ½" (1.3 cm) from edges. Trim seam allowances to scant ¼" (6 mm).

2) Cut bias tape to length of seam allowances around neck opening plus 1" (2.5 cm). Open one fold of bias tape. Pin bias tape to wrong side of cape along neck edge, aligning tape foldline to stitching line; extend bias tape ½" (6 mm) beyond edges at center front. Stitch on foldline.

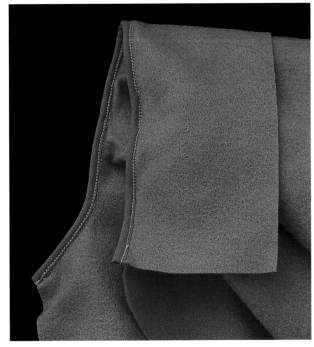

3) Turn under ½" (1.3 cm) of bias tape at each end. Fold bias tape over seam allowances; pin. Stitch close to tape edge, encasing seam allowances. Finger-press encased seam allowances toward cape; pin.

4) Cut ribbon for ties to desired length. Turn under ½" (1.3 cm) on one short end; pin to cape front, ½" (1.3 cm) from edge at center front, centering over neck seam. Stitch tie to cape, close to edges and along edge at center front as shown.

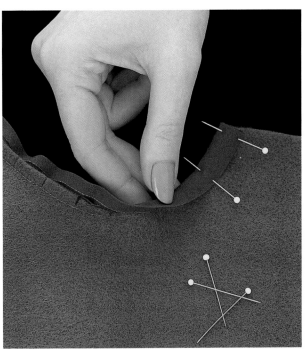

Cape without a collar. 1) Follow page 74, steps 1 to 3. Cut bias tape to length of neck opening plus 1" (2.5 cm). Open one fold of bias tape. Pin bias tape to right side of cape around neck edge, aligning raw edges; extend bias tape ½" (1.3 cm) beyond edges at center front. Stitch bias tape to neckline, stitching on foldline.

2) Press seam allowances toward bias tape. Clip the neck seam allowances as necessary. Turn under ½" (1.3 cm) of bias tape at each end. Fold bias tape to wrong side of cape; pin. Stitch close to remaining fold in bias tape. Follow step 4, above, pinning ties to center front at neck edge.

Skirts

Skirts are often a primary costume element. Instructions are given for several basic styles. The length of the skirts and amount of fullness can vary as appropriate for your particular costume. Choose from an elastic-waist skirt with an optional overlay (left) or a leaf or petal skirt (page 82).

Make the elastic-waist skirt in any length desired, using a fullness of two to four times the waist measurement. To add an overlay, select a fabric that does not ravel, such as tulle, or select a lace with a decorative lower edge. More fullness can be used in the optional overlay, depending on the look desired and the sheerness of the fabric. The skirt overlay can be embellished at the lower edge with sequin trim.

The leaf or petal skirt is constructed with foam for a firm, padded appearance. Design lines can be stitched onto the leaves to create veins.

Elastic-waist Skirt with Optional Overlay

✂ Cutting Directions

Cut one rectangle from the skirt fabric, with the length equal to the desired length of the skirt plus 1" (2.5 cm) for seam and hem allowances and the width equal to two to four times the waist measurement, depending on the desired fullness of the skirt.

For an overlay with equal fullness to the skirt, cut one rectangle from the overlay fabric, with the length equal to the desired length of the skirt plus ½" (1.3 cm). The cut width of the overlay fabric is equal to the cut width of the skirt fabric. For an overlay with added fullness, the cut length of the overlay fabric is equal to twice the desired skirt length plus 1" (2.5 cm). The cut width of the overlay fabric may be four to six times the waist measurement, depending on the weight of the fabric and the desired look. Seam fabric widths together in ⅜" (1 cm) seams, if necessary.

Cut a strip of skirt fabric for the elastic casing at the waist, with the length equal to the widest hip measurement plus 3" (7.5 cm) and the width equal to two times the width of the elastic plus 1¼" (3.2 cm).

YOU WILL NEED

Fabric, for skirt, amount depending on length and fullness of skirt.

Fabric, such as lace or tulle, for overlay, amount depending on length and fullness.

Elastic of desired width, for waist.

Decorative trim, for lower edge of overlay, optional. Amount needed is equal to the cut width of the overlay.

Lightweight cord, such as pearl cotton.

How to Sew an Elastic-waist Skirt

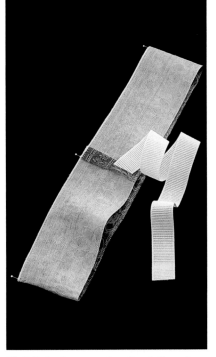

1) Stitch skirt widths together in ⅜" (1 cm) seams, forming continuous circle. Finish seams with overlock or zigzag stitch. Turn up ¼" (6 mm) twice to wrong side on lower edge of skirt. Stitch close to second fold.

2) Stitch short ends of waistband casing, right sides together, in ½" (1.3 cm) seam, leaving opening for inserting elastic. Press seam allowances open. Finish one long edge of waistband with overlock or zigzag stitch. Divide remaining long edge into quarters; pin-mark.

3) Zigzag over cord ⅜" (1 cm) from upper edge of skirt. Divide upper edge into quarters; pin-mark. Pin unfinished edge of waistband casing to upper edge of skirt, right sides together, matching pin marks. Pull up on cord to gather; distribute fullness evenly.

(Continued on next page)

4) Stitch ½" (1.3 cm) from raw edges. Trim seam allowances to ¼" (6 mm). Press seam allowances toward casing.

5) Fold casing to inside, overlapping stitching line ⅜" (1 cm); pin from right side, along the seamline. Stitch on right side of skirt, stitching in the ditch of the casing seam.

6) Cut elastic equal to waist measurement plus 1" (2.5 cm). Thread elastic through casing, using a safety pin or bodkin. Try on skirt, and mark elastic for a comfortable fit around waist. (Skirt is shown inside out, for ease in fitting.)

7) Cut elastic to desired length plus ½" (1.3 cm). Overlap ends of elastic ½" (1.3 cm). Stitch back and forth through both layers, using wide zigzag stitch or three-step zigzag stitch. Ease elastic back into casing. Stitch casing opening closed.

How to Sew a Skirt with an Overlay of Equal Fullness

1) Follow steps 1 and 2 on page 79. Stitch overlay widths together in ⅜" (1 cm) seams, forming long strip, for overlay with center front opening, or continuous circle. Stitch trim, if desired, to lower edge and open ends of overlay, using wide, long, zigzag stitch.

2) Pin wrong side of overlay to right side of skirt, along upper edge. Complete skirt, following steps 3 to 7 on pages 79 and 80.

How to Attach an Overlay with Added Fullness

1) Sew skirt as on pages 79 and 80, steps 1 to 5. Prepare overlay as in step 1, above, stitching trim to the lower edge only. Fold overlay fabric in half, forming two layers. Stitch two rows of gathering stitches within ½" (1.3 cm) of fold. Divide upper edges of skirt and overlay into quarters; pin-mark.

2) Pin the overlay to right side of skirt, matching marks and centering seamline of casing between gathering threads of the overlay. Pull up gathering threads, distributing fullness evenly. Stitch overlay to skirt, stitching over casing seamline. Complete skirt, following steps 6 and 7, opposite.

Leaf or Petal Skirt

✄ Cutting Directions

Cut a 3½" (9 cm) strip of fabric for the waistband, with the length equal to the waist measurement plus 2" to 4" (5 to 10 cm) for ease plus 3" (7.5 cm) for seam allowances and overlap.

Determine the number and size of the leaves or petals that will fit between the pin marks on the waistband, as marked in step 1, opposite. Draw a pattern for the leaf or petal, with the upper edge 1" (2.5 cm) wider than the desired finished width. Add ½" (1.3 cm) seam allowance around the entire pattern. Cut two pieces from fabric and one from foam, for each leaf or petal, using the pattern.

Wrap the elastic snugly around the waist; mark. Cut the elastic 3" (7.5 cm) longer than the marked length.

YOU WILL NEED

Fabric.

¼" (6 mm) foam, for petal or leaf interlining.

Waistband elastic, 1" (2.5 cm) wide.

Hook and loop tape.

How to Sew a Leaf or Petal Skirt

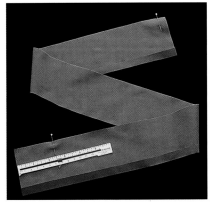

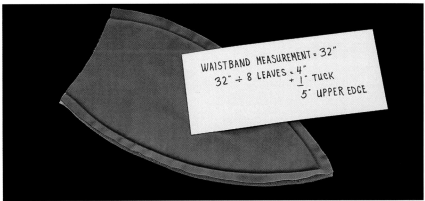

1) Press up ½" (1.3 cm) on one long edge of waistband. Pin-mark the opposite edge of waistband ½" (1.3 cm) from one end and 2½" (6.5 cm) from opposite end.

2) Layer pieces, right sides together, over the foam. Stitch ½" (1.3 cm) from raw edges, leaving upper edge open.

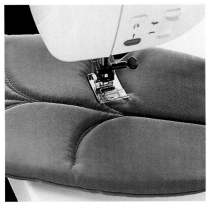

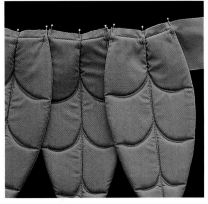

3) Trim seam allowances to scant ¼" (6 mm). Turn leaf or petal right side out; press. Baste upper raw edges together; trim out foam on upper edge.

4) Repeat steps 2 and 3 for all leaves or petals. Stitch any design lines. Fold ½" (1.3 cm) tuck at center of upper edge, folding out 1" (2.5 cm) of fabric; baste.

5) Pin leaves or petals to the edge of the waistband between pin marks, right sides together, matching raw edges; space leaves or petals evenly. Stitch ½" (1.3 cm) seam.

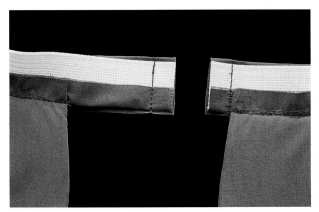

6) Fold waistband in half, right sides together; place elastic over waistband as shown. Stitch across waistband, ½" (1.3 cm) from ends, stitching through elastic. Turn right side out; press. Pin in the ditch of the seam. Stitch in the ditch, catching lower edge of waistband on back side.

7) Cut 2" (5 cm) length of hook and loop tape. Stitch hook side of tape to right side of extension. Stitch loop side of tape to wrong side of waistband at the opposite end.

Bat Wings

Select from two wing styles to give your bat or alien creature costume a dramatic finish. One wing style is made from fabric and is attached to the arms and legs, using loops of elastic. The other is made from felt and is buttoned to the costume along the lower edge of the sleeve and down the side of the garment. Both wing styles allow ease for stretching the arms outward. Instructions for creating the wing patterns are flexible, so you can adjust the spacing between the scallops along the outer edges of the wings and determine the best placement of elastic loops or buttons for securing the wings in place.

When making the fabric wing, you may wish to place the elastic loops at the wrist, shoulder, thigh, ankle, and a couple of inches to each side of the elbow and knee for ease of movement. For the felt wing, it is not necessary to space all the buttonholes at equal distances from each other. You may wish to space them closer together along the sleeve and upper body and farther apart along the leg. It may also be helpful to space two buttonholes close together at the underarm area to secure the wing close to the garment at this point.

The amount of fabric and ribbon needed for the wings depends on the size of the costume. It may be helpful to make the pattern before selecting the fabric.

Metallic brocade fabric is used to make an impressive set of wings for a young bat hero (opposite). Felt wings add fun to the playful bird-creature costume above.

✂ Cutting Directions

For fabric wings, cut two pieces for each wing, using the pattern as drawn on pages 86 and 87, steps 1 to 6.

For felt wings, cut one piece for each wing, using the pattern as drawn on page 87, steps 1 and 2.

YOU WILL NEED

Fabric wings:

Fabric; contrasting fabric may be used for wing back.

Elastic, ¼" to ½" (6 mm to 1.3 cm) wide.

Felt wings:

Felt.

Ribbon, ⅝" (1.5 cm) wide.

Buttons.

How to Draw the Pattern for Bat Wings

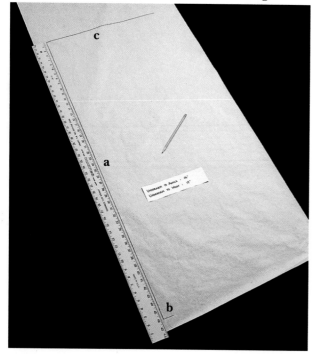

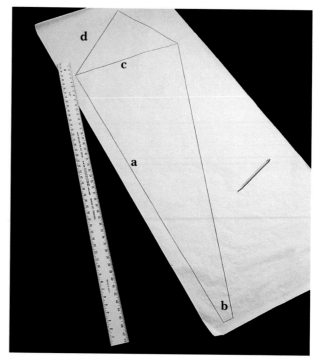

Fabric wings. 1) Draw line **(a)** on paper, with length equal to measurement from underarm to ankle. At ankle end, draw 1¼" (3.2 cm) line **(b)** perpendicular to line **(a)**. At underarm end, draw line **(c)** perpendicular to line **(a)**, with length equal to measurement from underarm to wrist.

2) Draw line **(d)** from underarm, at 45° angle from line **(c)**, with same length as line **(c)**. Draw lines connecting endpoints of lines **(b)**, **(c)**, and **(d)**, for outer edge of wing pattern.

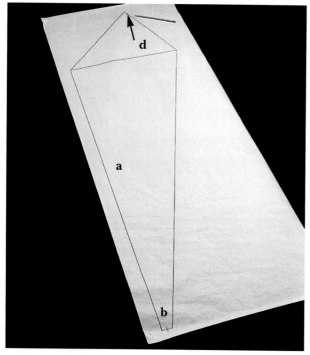

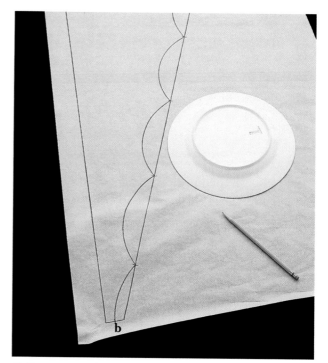

3) Mark point on line **(b)** ⅝" (1.5 cm) from line **(a)**. Mark another point on upper section of outer edge ⅝" (1.5 cm) from line **(d)**.

4) Determine desired scallop spacing of lower section of outer edge, planning scallop widths of 6" to 8" (15 to 20.5 cm), with lowest scallop slightly smaller than others. Draw scallops in lower section, drawing lowest scallop to marked point on line **(b)**.

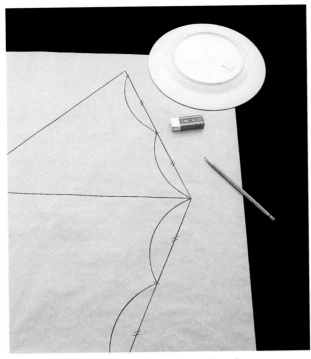

5) Draw one or two scallops along line for upper section of outer edge, from marked point to corner; for small size, draw one scallop; for larger size, divide section into two scallops. Disregard unnecessary lines along outer edge.

6) Add ½" (1.3 cm) seam allowances to all edges of pattern. Cut out pattern.

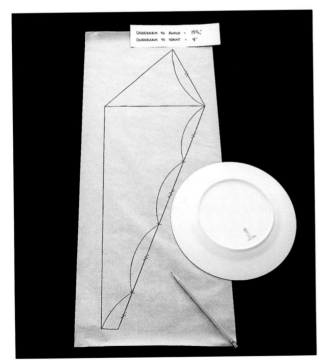

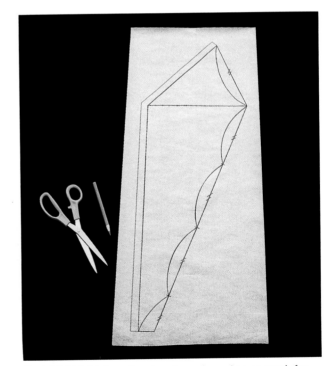

Felt wings. 1) Follow steps 1, 2, 4, and 5, opposite, omitting references to marked points and drawing scallops from ends of lines marking outer edge.

2) Add ⅝" (1.5 cm) extension along inner straight edge of wing pattern. Cut out pattern.

How to Sew Bat Wings from Fabric

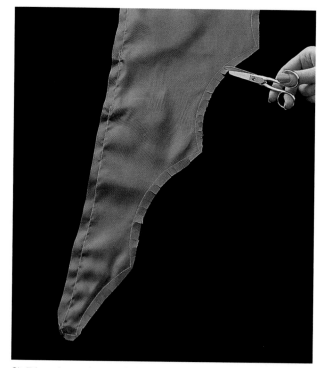

1) Determine placement of elastic loops for securing wings to arms and legs. Cut elastic to fit comfortably around arms and legs at desired points plus 1" (2.5 cm). Fold elastic lengths in half, and pin to right side of one wing piece at desired locations. Stitch elastic to seam allowances a scant ½" (1.3 cm) from raw edges.

2) Pin wing pieces right sides together, pinning elastic loops out of the way of seam allowances, if necessary; stitch ½" (1.3 cm) from raw edges, leaving about 6" (15 cm) opening on underarm-to-ankle side of wing for turning. Trim seam allowances. Trim points, and clip curves.

3) Turn wing right side out; press. Stitch opening closed. Mark lines on one side of wing, from underarm to points on outer edge. Pin layers together along marked lines.

4) Stitch on marked lines through both layers. Fold wing front sides together on stitched line; press fold. Stitch close to fold, making pintuck. Repeat for all stitched lines.

How to Sew Bat Wings from Felt

1) **Fold** wing, front sides together, from underarm to first point on outer edge of wing; press fold. Stitch close to fold, making a pintuck. Repeat for all but last point on outer edge of wing.

2) **Pin** ribbon to front side of wing, along inner straight edges, from wrist to ankle, pinning a tuck at underarm and turning under about ⅜" (1 cm) at each end. Stitch close to edges of ribbon.

3) **Mark** placement of buttonholes on ribbon, spacing as necessary to hold wing securely to garment. Make buttonholes.

4) **Try on** costume; mark button positions. Stitch buttons to costume.

Padded Wings

Padded wings can be used for costumes such as angels, birds, butterflies, or other winged creatures. The wings are designed with a layer of foam between layers of fabric. Wire may be stitched around the outer seam allowances to help support the shape of the wings.

To create wings that sparkle, make the wings from fabrics with metallic threads. Or use a base fabric and cover it with a transparent overlay of glitter organza, glitter tulle, or sparkle mesh. Simply pin the overlay pieces, right side up, to the right sides of all the wing pieces, and baste them together ⅜" (1 cm) from the outer edges. Then sew the wings as on pages 92 and 93, steps 1 to 6. Wings may also be embellished with appliquéd designs, if desired.

Padded wings can be designed in any shape and size to suit the needs of the costume, provided each wing is no wider than the width of the foam. Simply draw a pattern on paper for one wing, to the size and shape desired. For best results, plan to join the wings in a straight center seam at least 6" (15 cm) long. You may use any of the wing designs shown here or develop your own style. Add a ½" (1.3 cm) seam allowance to the entire outer edge of the pattern.

Wings can be worn is a variety of ways. They can be sewn directly to the back of another part of the costume, such as a tabard or full suit. Wings can be made detachable, using hook and loop tape. Or an elastic harness that fits over the shoulders can be sewn to the wings. When worn with a gown, an opening in the back of the gown allows the harness to be hidden.

✂ Cutting Directions

Cut four wing pieces, two for the fronts and two for the backs.

For a transparent overlay, cut four wing pieces from transparent fabric.

Cut two wing pieces from ¼" (6 mm) foam. Trim ½" (1.3 cm) seam allowance from center edges.

YOU WILL NEED

Fabric, for wings.
Fabric, for wing overlay, optional.
Foam, ¼" (6 mm) thick, for padded wings.
Silicone lubricant, for ease in sewing over foam, optional.
19-gauge wire, for wings with wired edges.
Hook and loop tape, for attaching wings, optional.
Elastic, ½" (1.3 cm) wide, for harness.

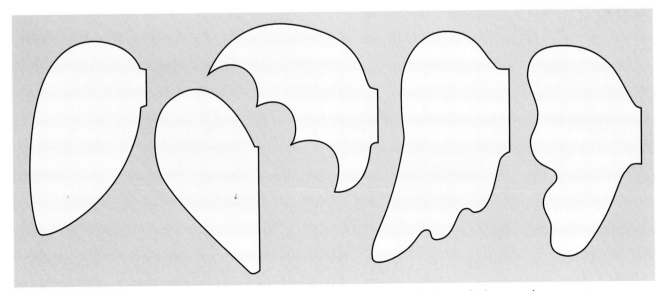

Wings appear in nature and fantasy in a wide range of shapes and sizes. Select a design to suit your costume, or draw a shape, following the guidelines above.

How to Sew Padded Wings

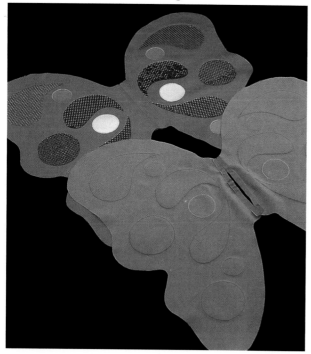

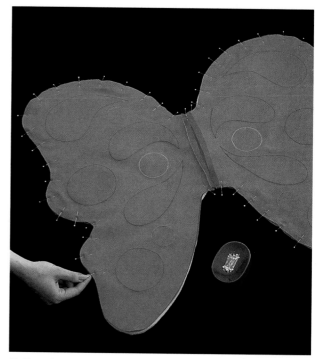

1) Apply any surface embellishments that should be done before construction, such as appliqués (page 30). Pin wing back pieces, right sides together, along center back; stitch ½" (1.3 cm) seam. Press seam allowances open. Repeat for wing front pieces, leaving 6" (15 cm) opening in seam for turning.

2) Lay foam on flat surface, butting center edges. Place wing front over wing back, right sides together; then place over foam. Pin. Stitch ½" (1.3 cm) from outer edges. Apply silicone lubricant to bed of the machine to help foam feed evenly. For wings without wired edges, omit steps 3 and 4.

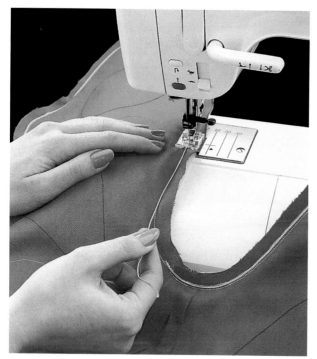

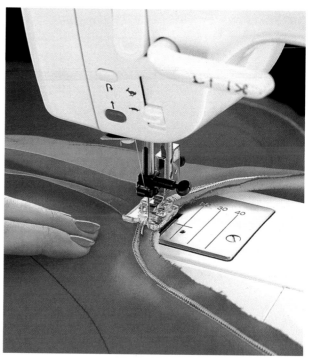

3) Set machine for zigzag sitch with medium width and short stitch length. Place the wire just outside previous stitching; stitch over wire around the entire outer edge in a continuous circle, using a 90/14 needle and a presser foot with recessed bottom.

4) Cut the wire, overlapping ends about 2" (5 cm). Zigzag over overlapped ends, using closely spaced stitches to secure.

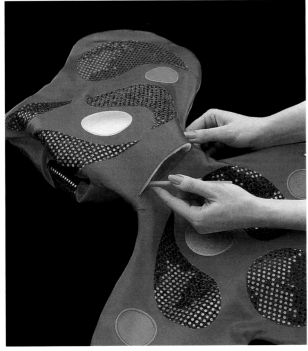

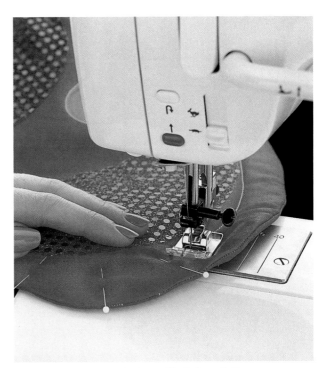

5) Trim seam allowances to ¼" (6 mm). Clip curves and trim points. Turn wings right side out through center front seam opening. Push out points of wings, using the eraser end of a pencil. Press lightly; hand-stitch opening closed.

6) Topstitch around wings 1" (2.5 cm) from outer edges. Stitch any additional design lines as desired. Sew wings to back of costume, if desired, or attach elastic harness, below.

How to Sew an Elastic Harness

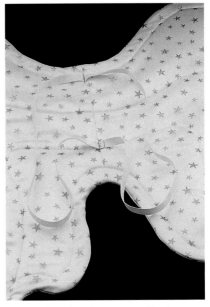

1) Wrap the elastic from the center back over one shoulder and return to the center back; pull the elastic comfortably snug. Mark point of intersection.

2) Cut elastic twice the length from end to mark. Overlap the ends ½" (1.3 cm), forming circle. Stitch back and forth through both layers, using wide zigzag stitch or three-step zigzag stitch.

3) Pin the elastic perpendicular to the center seam of wings, with top of elastic circle at the top of seam and bottom of circle 2" to 6" (5 to 15 cm) below, forming two loops of equal size. Sew across elastic several times to secure.

Sheer Wings

Sheer wings are especially suitable for insect costumes. They can be made from any sheer fabric and are supported with wire around the outer edges. Sheer wings work best when made on a small scale, with each wing measuring no wider than 15" (38 cm) across.

Draw the wings in one large piece, with a flat section between the wings that measures 2" (5 cm) wide and 4" to 6" (10 to 15 cm) long. Keep outer edges gently rounded, avoiding any sharp curves.

✂ Cutting Directions

Cut a piece of sheer fabric and a piece of stabilizer as on page 96, step 1.

Cut a 4" (10 cm) strip of medium-weight fabric for the center support, with the length equal to twice the length of the center flat section of the wings plus 1" (2.5 cm). Cut a piece of 1/4" (6 mm) foam 1 7/8" (4.7 cm) wide, with the length equal to the length of the center flat section of the wings.

YOU WILL NEED

Tear-away stabilizer or wide paper, such as freezer paper.

19-gauge wire, available at hardware stores, or heavy-gauge milliner's wire, available at fabric stores.

Sheer fabric.

Mediumweight fabric, in color to match wings, and 1/4" (6 mm) foam, for center support.

Elastic, 1/2" (1.3 cm) wide, for harness, optional.

Hook and loop tape, for attaching wings, optional.

How to Sew Sheer Wings

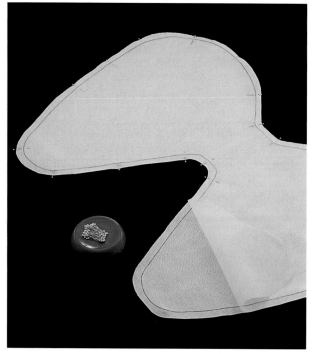

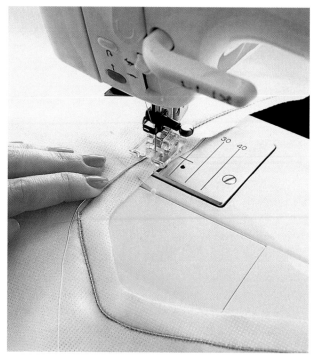

1) Draw the desired shape for wings on tear-away stabilizer or wide paper. Pin sheer fabric over the stabilizer. Cut out both layers, leaving ½" (1.3 cm) margin around outer edge. Pin sheer fabric to stabilizer along entire outer edge.

2) Set machine for zigzag stitch with medium width and short length. Place the wire over fabric along marked line, beginning at center flat section; stitch over wire around entire outer edge in a continuous circle, using presser foot with recessed bottom.

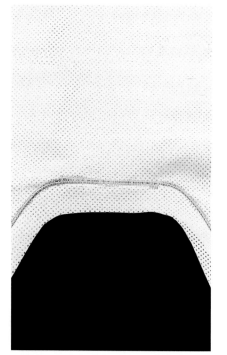

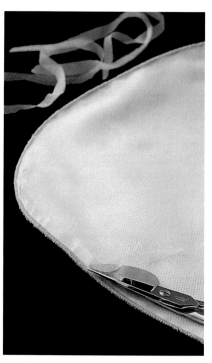

3) Cut wire, overlapping ends about 2" (5 cm). Zigzag over overlapped ends, using closely spaced stitches to secure.

4) Trim away stabilizer carefully around outer edge. Set machine for satin stitch. Turn excess fabric back over wire. Satin stitch over fabric-covered wire around entire outer edge.

5) Trim away excess fabric up to the stitches. Carefully tear away remaining stabilizer.

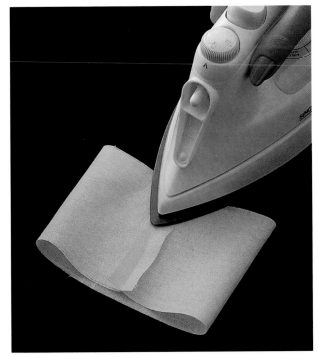

6) Fold center support strip in half crosswise, right sides together; stitch ½" (1.3 cm) from raw edges, forming circle. Press seam open.

7) Fold in raw edges of support, butting at center; press. Insert foam strip under the folds on side of support opposite seam.

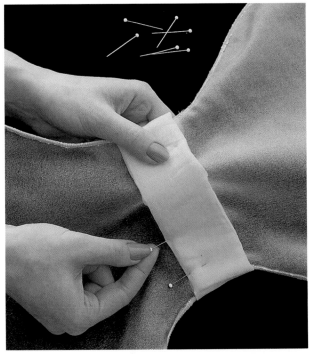

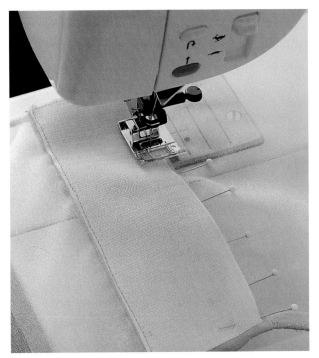

8) Slip one wing through support, and center padded front over flat space between wings. If wings will be worn with elastic harness, prepare the harness as on page 93, steps 1 and 2. Slip harness through back of support; pin, spacing elastic as in step 3. Align front and back outer edges of support; pin.

9) Edgestitch along outer edges on front of support, catching back of support and harness, if used, in the stitching. For wings without harness, sew wings to back of costume, or sew hook side of hook and loop tape to back of support; sew loop side of tape to costume.

Finishing Touches

Collars

An imaginative collar can be an expressive costume element. The fabric, shape, and details can be varied to make a collar suitable for any creature or character.

Either of two basic collar styles can be sewn to suit the needs of the costume. A flat collar can be designed with a uniquely shaped outer edge and accented with topstitched design lines, if desired. For added shaping, it can be padded with foam interlining.

A gathered collar is a suitable accent for a fairy or ballerina costume or for any type of plant costume. For this collar style, use fabrics that do not ravel easily. Nylon knit fabrics or tulle work well.

Padded flat collar, suitable for a superhero (above), is sewn from metallic fabric and accented with stitched design lines. The lion's mane (opposite) is a plush felt flat collar. The fairy wears a frilly, two-layered gathered collar.

✂ Cutting Directions

For a flat collar, make the pattern as on page 102, steps 1 to 4. Cut two collar pieces from fabric, using the pattern. For a padded flat collar, also cut one collar piece from foam, using the pattern.

For a gathered collar, cut one rectangle from fabric, with the length equal to the measurement of the neck at the base of the neck times three and the width equal to the desired length of the collar plus ½" (1.3 cm). Cut one 2¾" (7 cm) strip for the binding, equal to the length of the neck measurement plus 2" (5 cm), cutting the strip on the bias for woven fabrics or on the crosswise grain for knit fabrics.

YOU WILL NEED

Flat collar:

Fabric, amount depending on size of collar.

¼" (6 mm) foam, for padded collar.

Hook and eye closure.

Gathered collar:

Fabric, for collar, about one collar length for neck sizes 15" (38 cm) and smaller.

Fabric, for binding, about ⅛ yd. (0.15 m) for crosswise grain or about ⅜ yd. (0.35 m) for bias grain.

Hook and eye closure.

How to Draw a Pattern for a Flat Collar

1) Cut rectangle of paper larger than the desired finished size of collar. Fold paper in half lengthwise, then crosswise. Measure neck and mark arc on paper as on page 74, step 1.

2) Cut out neck opening. Unfold paper; slash on one fold to neck opening, for center back seam.

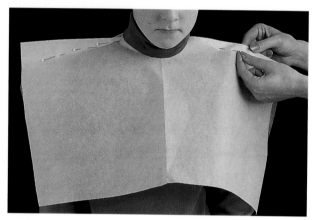

3) Slip pattern around neck, butting edges of slash at center back; tape, using removable tape. Fold out equal amounts of excess paper at shoulder folds, allowing pattern to conform to shape of shoulders; pin.

4) Remove pattern; fold in half along center front. Adjust neckline curve, if necessary. Draw desired collar shape; add ½" (1.3 cm) seam allowance along outer edge. Cut out pattern. Try on pattern to check fit.

How to Sew a Flat Collar

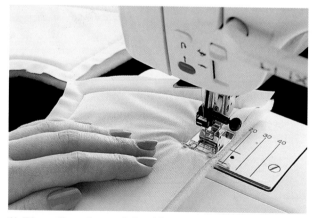

1) Pin collar pieces right sides together. For a padded collar, place the collar pieces over foam; pin. Stitch around all sides, ½" (1.3 cm) from raw edges, leaving opening on one center back seam or along one straight edge of collar, for turning.

2) Trim seam allowances close to stitching. Clip any corners or curves. Turn collar right side out; press. Slipstitch opening closed. Stitch any design lines on collar as desired. Stitch hook and eye to center back at neck edge.

How to Sew a Gathered Collar

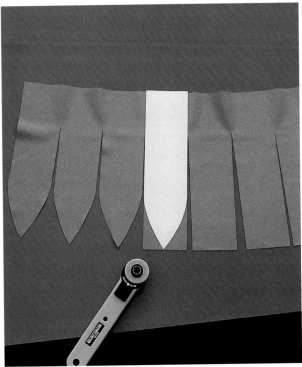

1) Cut slashes on one long edge of rectangle, about 2" (5 cm) apart, cutting slashes to about 2" (5 cm) from opposite long side. Trim end of each slashed strip of fabric to a point.

2) Stitch two rows of gathering stitches within ½" (1.3 cm) seam allowance on remaining long edge of fabric. Pull gathering threads, gathering fabric to measurement of neck at base of neck plus 1" (2.5 cm).

3) Press binding strip in half, wrong sides together. Pin-mark ½" (1.3 cm) from each end. Pin right side of gathered collar to binding strip between the pin marks, arranging gathers evenly along strip. Stitch ½" (1.3 cm) seam; trim to ¼" (6 mm).

4) Turn under ½" (1.3 cm) at ends of binding. Wrap binding to back side, just covering stitching; pin in the ditch of the seam. Stitch in the ditch on the right side, catching the binding on the back side. Slipstitch ends. Stitch hook and eye to ends of collar.

Arm & Leg Accents

Armbands or gathered wristlets and anklets can give added flourish to simple costumes. Gathered wristlets or anklets can be made to accompany a gathered collar for a fairy princess costume. Or, for any plant costume, they can be made to look like clumps of leaves. Padded armbands, much like spats and hoods, give the costume a larger-than-life appearance. They can be designed with appliqués (page 30) or other surface embellishments to coordinate them with the rest of the costume. Vent hose armbands are a wonderful addition to a robot costume. They are made from flexible vinyl vent hose, which can be purchased at any hardware store in a range of sizes. Select a hose that comfortably fits over the arm. A larger diameter hose can be used to make leggings.

✂ Cutting Directions

For gathered wristlets, cut two strips of fabric, with the length equal to three times the wrist measurement and the width equal to the measurement from the wrist to the knuckles plus ½" (1.3 cm) for seam allowance. Cut two 2¾" (7 cm) bias strips of fabric for the elastic casing, with the length equal to the wrist measurement plus 3" (7.5 cm). Cut two pieces of ¼" (6 mm) elastic, with the length equal to the wrist measurement plus ½" (1.3 cm).

For gathered anklets, cut two strips of fabric, with the length equal to three times the ankle measurement and the width equal to the measurement from the ankle to the floor plus ½" (1.3 cm) for the seam allowance. Cut two 2¾" (7 cm) bias strips of fabric for the elastic casing, with the length equal to the ankle measurement plus 4" (10 cm). Cut two pieces of ¼" (6 mm) elastic, with the length equal to the ankle measurement plus ½" (1.3 cm).

For padded armbands, cut two armbands, two lining pieces, and two pieces of foam interlining, using the pattern drawn on page 107, steps 1 and 2. Cut hook and loop tape, with the length equal to the finished length of the opening minus ¼" (6 mm).

For vent hose armbands or leggings covered with two-way stretch fabric, cut one rectangle of fabric, with the width equal to the measurement around the vent hose and the length equal to the desired length of the armband or legging plus 4" (10 cm). If using tricot-backed lamé, cut one rectangle of fabric, with the width equal to the measurement around the vent hose plus 1" (2.5 cm) for seam allowances and the length equal to the desired length of the armband or legging plus 4" (10 cm).

Gathered wristlets and padded armbands (opposite) complement gathered collars (page 100) and flat, padded collars (page 101). Vent hose armbands and leggings (above) enhance a robot costume.

YOU WILL NEED

Gathered wristlets or anklets:
Fabric.
¼" (6 mm) elastic.

Padded armbands:
Fabric.
¼" (6 mm) foam, for interlining.
Hook and loop tape.

Vent hose armbands or leggings:
Vinyl vent hose, with diameter large enough to fit over arms or legs.
Masking tape.
Wire cutter.
Metallic two-way stretch fabric, or tricot-backed lamé.
¼" (6 mm) elastic.

How to Sew Gathered Wristlets or Anklets

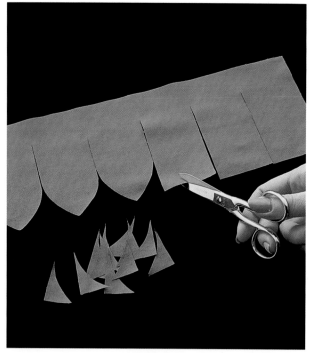

1) Cut slashes on one long edge of fabric strip, about 2" (5 cm) apart, cutting slashes to about 1" (2.5 cm) from opposite edge. Trim the end of each slashed section to a point.

2) Stitch two rows of gathering stitches within ½" (1.3 cm) seam allowance on remaining long edge of fabric.

3) Stitch short ends of casing strip, right sides together, ½" (1.3 cm) from ends, forming circle; press seam open. Press casing in half, wrong sides together. Pin right side of slashed strip to casing, pulling up on threads to gather the strip; butt ends of gathered strip at seamline of casing. Arrange gathers evenly.

4) Stitch ½" (1.3 cm) seam; trim to ¼" (6 mm). Wrap casing to back side, just covering stitching; pin in the ditch of the seam.

5) Stitch in the ditch on the right side, catching the lower edge of the casing on the back side. Leave 1" (2.5 cm) opening for inserting elastic.

6) Insert elastic through opening, using safety pin. Overlap ends ½" (1.3 cm); stitch securely. Stitch opening closed.

How to Draw a Pattern for Padded Armbands

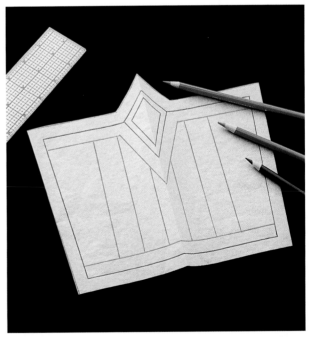

1) Draw rectangle on tracing paper, with length equal to desired length of the band plus 1½" (3.8 cm) and width equal to measurement around arm at wide end of the band plus 3¾" (9.5 cm). Fold paper in half lengthwise. Mark point at wrist end a distance from fold equal to half of wrist measurement plus 1⅞" (4.7 cm). Draw line from point to upper corner.

2) Shape the pattern at upper and lower edges, if desired. Cut on line; unfold pattern. Draw seamlines ½" (1.3 cm) to inside of cut edges. Mark placement of any appliqués and design lines. Try on pattern to check fit.

How to Sew Padded Armbands

1) Apply any surface embellishments that should be done before construction, such as appliqués (page 30). Pin armband and lining, right sides together, over foam interlining. Stitch ½" (1.3 cm) from raw edges, leaving 3" (7.5 cm) opening for turning.

2) Fold back upper layer at opening; stitch lower layer to foam, scant ½" (1.3 cm) from raw edges. Trim seam allowances; trim corners.

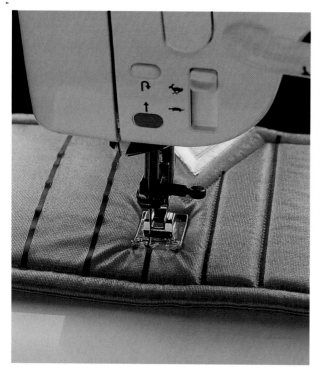

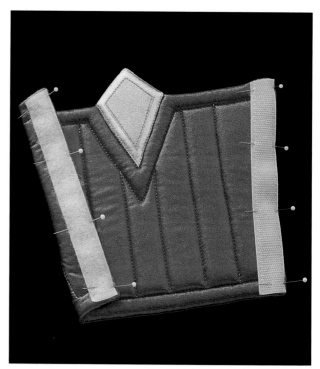

3) Turn armband right side out; press. Slipstitch opening closed. Topstitch along upper and lower edges only. Stitch any design lines on armbands.

4) Pin hook side of tape to outside of armband, close to one opening edge. Pin loop side of tape to inside of armband, close to opposite edge; stitch close to all edges of tape. Repeat for other armband, lapping opening edges in opposite direction.

How to Make Vent Hose Armbands or Leggings

1) Cut vent hose to desired length of armband or legging; cut wire, using wire cutter. At end of hose, trim the vinyl and fold wire end back 1" (2.5 cm); crimp with pliers. Tape end securely to adjacent wire. Repeat for all ends.

2) Fold fabric in half lengthwise, right sides together; pin long edges. Stitch ½" (1.3 cm) seam, using narrow zigzag stitch. Turn under ½" (1.3 cm) casing at ends. Stitch ⅜" (1 cm) from the fold, using narrow zigzag stitch; leave opening for inserting elastic.

3) Measure arm or leg at desired location for lower elastic. Cut two pieces of elastic, with lengths equal to this measurement plus 1" (2.5 cm). Insert elastic into lower casing; adjust for comfortable fit. Overlap ends; stitch securely. Stitch openings closed.

4) Insert vent hose into fabric tubes, sliding the hose to elasticized end of tube. Repeat step 3 for upper elastic, measuring at desired location on upper arm or leg. Center hose in fabric tube; tack ends in place.

Gloves

Give the finishing touch to your costume with a pair of custom-designed gloves. Make an animal paw, complete with claws, from an inexpensive work glove. Paint a pair of garden gloves to match a robot or space suit costume. Or simply add long, painted fingernails to a plain black nylon or cotton glove to coordinate with a bat or witch costume.

Begin with an inexpensive pair of gloves, and add stitched or painted embellishments and plastic nail tips as appropriate for your costume. Purchase nail tips in the cosmetics section of drugstores, or find specialty nail tips at costume shops. Follow manufacturers' recommendations and warnings, since nail tip glues will bond to skin in a few seconds. Look for black, brown, green, or glow-in-the-dark fingernail polish to give the nail tips the perfect finish.

Tips for Embellishing Gloves

Paint inexpensive gloves with aerosol paint to match costume.

Stitch beads, buttons, or other found objects to gloves. If desired, paint found objects to match gloves before securing in place.

Fuse scraps of fabric to top of gloves, using paper-backed fusible web. Follow manufacturer's directions for fusing.

Draw designs on gloves, using paint in fine-tipped tubes. Or create designs on gloves, using colored glue. Allow paint and glue to dry thoroughly.

YOU WILL NEED

Gloves.

Animal paws:

Plush felt or synthetic fur scraps.

Raw edge accent:

¼" (6 mm) foam.

Nonraveling fabric scraps.

Padded fabric accent:

Fabric scraps.

Fusible interfacing.

¼" (6 mm) foam.

Nails or claws:

Plastic nail tips, in desired length; nail glue.

Fingernail polish, of desired color.

Wooden dowel, ⅜" to ½" (1 to 1.3 cm) in diameter.

Plastic sandwich bag.

How to Make an Animal Paw Glove

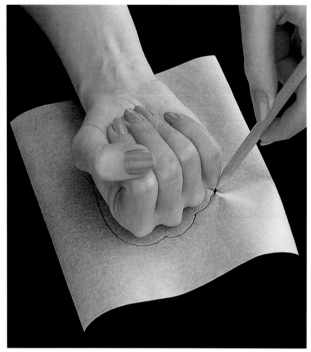

1) **Clench** fist, and position on paper as shown. Trace around the fist, eliminating thumb. Cut just inside marked lines to make pattern for fur patch on upper paw. Cut two fur patches, reversing the pattern for one to make a right and left patch.

2) **Glue** fur patch to top of glove, using fabric glue. Repeat for remaining glove. Apply claws as in steps 1 to 3, opposite, if desired.

How to Make a Glove with Raw-edge Fabric Accent

1) **Cut** desired shape from nonraveling fabric to fit over top of glove, using scissors or pinking shears. Cut piece of foam slightly larger than fabric shape. Pin fabric over foam; stitch ¼" (6 mm) from outer edges of fabric.

2) **Stitch** design lines over padded fabric shape as desired. Trim excess foam close to stitching. Hand-stitch accent to top of glove along outer stitching line. Apply nails or claws (opposite), if desired.

How to Make a Glove with a Padded Fabric Accent

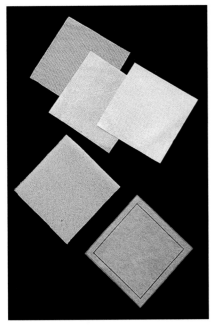  

1) Draw desired shape for padded accent on paper; add ¼" (6 mm) seam allowances to all sides. Cut two pieces from fabric, one from foam, and one from interfacing. Apply interfacing to wrong side of one fabric piece, following manufacturer's directions.

2) Layer fabric pieces, right sides together, over foam, with interfaced piece on top; pin. Stitch ¼" (6 mm) from raw edges. Cut small opening in top layer of fabric for turning. Trim corners. Turn right side out through opening; press.

3) Topstitch around outer edges of design. Stitch additional design lines on accent as desired. Hand-stitch accent to top of glove along outer design line. Apply nails or claws as below, if desired.

How to Apply Nails or Claws to Gloves

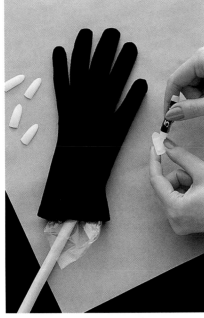  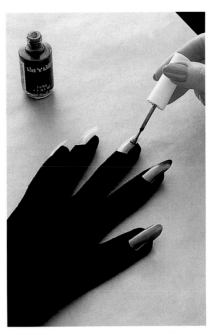

1) Trim nail tips as desired. Wrap the dowel with plastic sandwich bag; insert into thumb of glove. Apply glue liberally to lower half of nail tip.

2) Press nail tip in place over the dowel; hold for about 30 seconds. Move dowel to next finger; apply glue to nail tip, and press in place. Repeat for all nails. Allow nails to dry thoroughly.

3) Apply two or three coats of nail polish to nails, if desired, allowing nails to dry between coats.

Spats

Padded spats are an effective addition to costumes of all kinds. Worn over shoes, they can be made to look like metallic boots for a robot or an astronaut, or like oversized animal feet and paws. Foam interlining gives the spats enough body to stand up on the leg. A hook-and-loop-tape closure up the back makes them easy to put on and take off, while an elastic strap under the shoe helps to hold them in place.

✂Cutting Directions

Draw the pattern as in steps 1 to 5, below and on page 116. Cut two pieces from fabric, two from lining, two from foam, and two from interfacing, if desired, for each pair of spats.

Cut two pieces of ¼" (6 mm) elastic, with the length equal to the width of the shoe at the instep plus ½" (1.3 cm).

YOU WILL NEED

Fabric, for spats and lining.

¼" (6 mm) foam, for spats interlining.

Lightweight fusible interfacing, optional.

Elastic, ¼" (6 mm) wide.

Hook and loop tape.

Plastic nail tips, fingernail polish, glue, for animal spats with claws.

Silicone lubricant, for ease in sewing over foam, optional.

How to Draw a Pattern for Spats

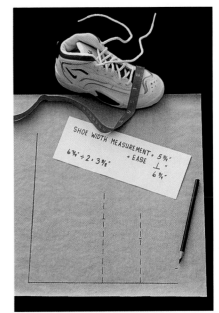

1) Measure the circumference of shoe sole; add 1" (2.5 cm) for ease, and divide by 2. Draw a line of this length on paper, for lower edge of pattern. Draw a line perpendicular to this line, with the length equal to desired finished length, for back of spat.

2) Draw a dotted line perpendicular to lower edge, marking the midpoint. Measure distance from floor over arch of shoe at highest point; add 1" (2.5 cm) for ease, and divide by 2. Mark a point on dotted line this distance from lower edge.

3) Draw a second dotted line, halfway between the midpoint and toe. Measure distance from floor over widest part of shoe at base of toes; add 1" (2.5 cm) for ease, and divide by 2. Mark a point on second dotted line this distance from lower edge. Mark a point 1" (2.5 cm) above toe-end of lower edge.

(Continued on next page)

How to Draw a Pattern for Spats (continued)

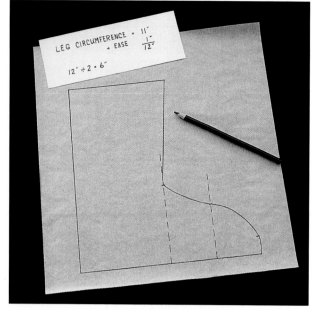

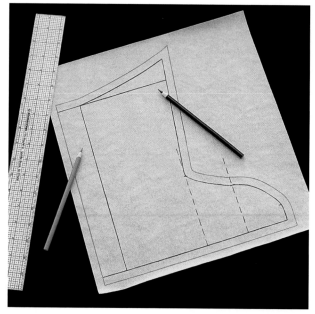

4) Measure distance around leg at desired height of spat; add 1" (2.5 cm) for ease, and divide by 2. Draw line for upper edge with this length, parallel to lower edge. Draw center front seamline, from front of upper edge to front of lower edge, intersecting marked points; curve line gently as shown.

5) Draw a line parallel to back of spat, 1½" (3.8 cm) from existing line; extend upper and lower edges to meet this line. Shape lower edge to make toes or claws, if desired. Shape upper edge, if desired. Add ½" (1.3 cm) seam allowance around upper, lower, and center front edges of spat pattern. Cut out pattern.

How to Sew Spats

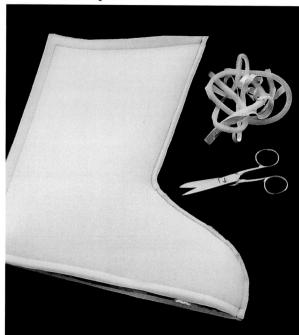

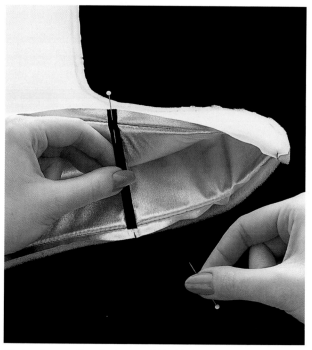

1) Fuse interfacing to wrong side of spat pieces, if desired, following manufacturer's directions. Pin one spat piece, right side up, to foam interlining; baste ⅜" (1 cm) from raw edges. Repeat for second spat piece. Pin two interlined spat pieces, right sides together, along center front. Stitch ½" (1.3 cm) seam. Trim seam; clip curves.

2) Apply appliqués (page 30), if desired. Pin elastic to right side of spat at instep, aligning ends of elastic to edges of spat. Stitch securely, ⅜" (1 cm) from edges.

3) Stitch two lining pieces, right sides together, along center front, using ½" (1.3 cm) seam allowance. Trim seam; clip curves.

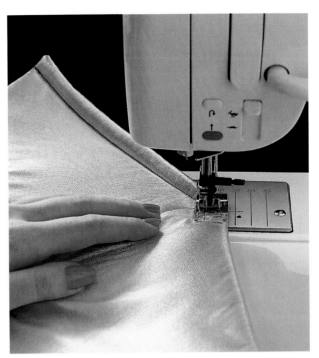

4) Pin spat to lining, right sides together; stitch ½" (1.3 cm) seam, leaving opening along one center back seam for turning. Trim seam. Turn right side out; press lightly. Slipstitch opening closed. Topstitch ½" (1.3 cm) from upper and lower edges.

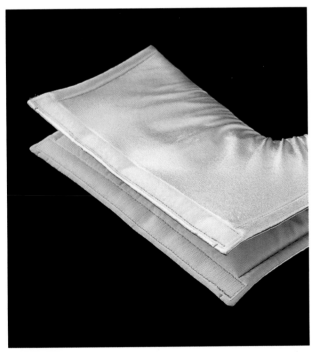

5) Pin hook side of hook and loop tape to wrong side of spat, ⅛" (3 mm) from one center back edge. Pin loop side of tape to right side of spat center back, ⅛" (3 mm) from opposite edge. Stitch around outer edges of tapes.

6) Repeat steps 1 to 5 for second spat, lapping the closure in opposite direction. Stitch any design lines on spats as desired. Add any surface embellishments.

Wands & Scepters

Props are often an effective addition to the costume. Just as every witch needs a broom, every wizard, magician, or fairy needs a wand and every king or queen needs a scepter. Wands and scepters are easily made from wooden dowels topped with padded fabric stars and glitzy streamers or with Styrofoam® balls and small finials. A little paint and some sparkling trims add a magical touch.

Hologram or glow-in-the-dark stickers are effective accents for magician and wizard wands. Celestial stickers are often available at science museums, children's toy stores, or party supply stores. Plastic gemstones to decorate a royal scepter can be purchased at craft and fabric stores.

YOU WILL NEED

All styles:

Craft acrylic paint and paintbrush.

Hot glue gun and glue sticks.

Star wand:

Fabric; lightweight fusible interfacing.

¼" (6 mm) foam, for interlining.

Metallic trim, optional.

⅜" (1 cm) wooden dowel, about 18" (46 cm) long.

Decorative trims, such as beads, ribbons, and decorative cords.

Magician or wizard wand:

Dense Styrofoam ball, about 2½" to 3" (6.5 to 7.5 cm) in diameter.

⅜" (1 cm) wooden dowel, about 18" (46 cm) long.

Stickers.

Royal scepter:

½" (1.3 cm) wooden dowel, 36" (91.5 cm) long.

Dense Styrofoam ball, 4" to 6" (10 to 15 cm) in diameter.

Macramé bead, doll pin stand, finial, available at craft stores.

Assorted plastic gemstones; glue.

A sparkling scepter or an enchanting wand (opposite) adds to the magic of make-believe. Glow-in-the-dark stickers and trims (right) create an aura of mystery.

How to Make a Star Wand

1) **Cut** two pieces of fabric and one piece of foam, larger than desired finished size of star. Apply fusible interfacing to wrong sides of fabric, following manufacturer's directions.

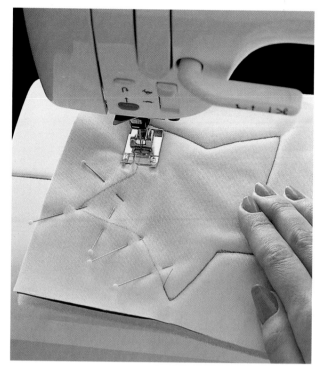

2) **Draw** or trace a star shape in desired size onto interfaced side of one fabric piece. Layer the fabric pieces, right sides together, over the foam, with star outline on top; pin. Stitch around star, leaving about 3" (7.5 cm) opening on one side for turning.

3) **Trim** fabric and foam close to stitching. Trim points; clip corners. Turn star right side out; press. Slipstitch opening closed. Topstitch around outer edges. Hand-stitch metallic trim to front of star over stitching line, if desired.

4) **Cut** trims into desired lengths. Bundle trims, and tie together at center; secure to back of star. Paint dowel handle; allow to dry. Secure handle over trims on back of star, using hot glue.

How to Make a Magician or Wizard Wand

1) Sand Styrofoam® ball lightly with sandpaper; wipe with damp rag to remove any powder residue. Poke hole large enough to fit dowel; insert dowel into ball about 1½" (3.8 cm), securing with hot glue.

2) Apply acrylic paint to ball and dowel; allow to dry. Apply stickers as desired. Embellish the handle, if desired.

How to Make a Royal Scepter

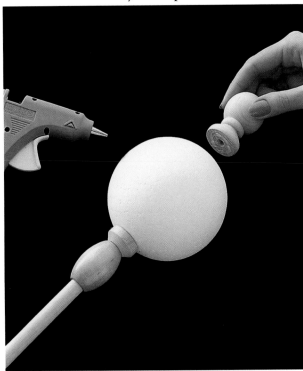

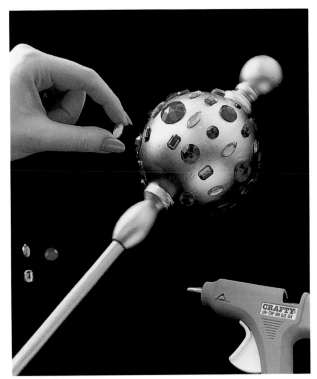

1) Follow step 1, above, using ½" (1.3 cm) dowel and larger ball. Secure any beads, doll pin stands, or finials to top and bottom of ball, using hot glue.

2) Apply acrylic paint to ball, bead, doll pin stand, finial, and dowel; allow to dry. Secure gemstones to ball as desired, using hot glue.

Face Painting

Water-based face paints are a safe, easy way to add character and personality to the costume. Because they are water-based, they are nontoxic, easy to apply, and removable with soap and water. Face paint kits, available in palette form, usually contain several basic colors plus black and white. Paints can also be purchased in individual pots. The colors may be used as they are or mixed to create any color desired.

Apply background colors to the entire face, using a damp foam makeup sponge. Begin with lighter colors first. Add shading as desired and apply details, using synthetic artist's brushes, makeup brushes, or cotton swabs.

Glitter paint, available in gel or stick form, can be used to add a little sparkle to the face. To avoid irritation, the glitter paint should not be applied too close to the eyes. Before using any of the paints on the face, it is a good idea to apply a small amount on the inside of the elbow or wrist to test for skin irritation. Read and follow the manufacturer's directions for use of their product.

Tips for Face Painting

Arrange all materials before starting to paint. Have plenty of clean water on hand for rinsing sponges and brushes.

Draw the face design on paper, using colored pencils, and follow your design as you paint.

Practice sponging and brushing techniques on the inside of your forearm.

Start with a clean face, free of makeup or lotion.

Apply light colors before dark colors.

Look up when painting under the eyes. Close the eyelids when painting them, and allow them to dry before opening them.

Shade areas under cheekbones and along chin and forehead, to emphasize the bone structure of the face.

How to Use Face Paint

1) Wet sponge; wring out excess water. Load paint onto sponge, rubbing sponge in circular motion over paint.

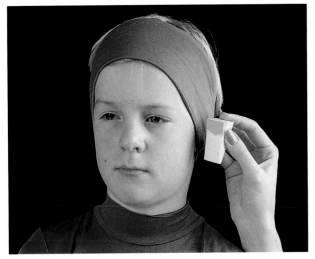

2) Apply base coat evenly to entire face, using a dabbing motion. Work paint gently into creases around nose, chin, and eyes; allow to dry. To make base color less transparent, apply a second base coat over first coat.

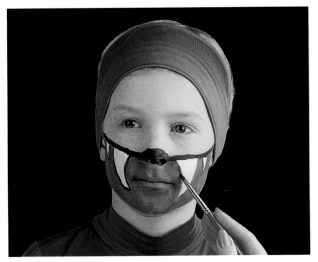

3) Paint the design features with an artist's brush, painting all areas of the same color before switching to another color. Allow paint to dry before painting over it with another color.

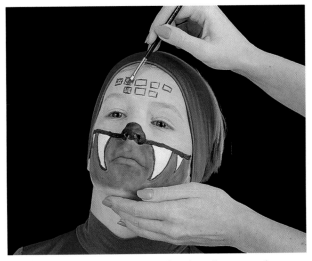

4) Apply glitter gel to desired painted areas, after paint has dried.

Yellow paint accents the face of this zinnia, creating the center of the bloom. A painted dragon-fly adds to the effect.

Glitter gel applied along the cheekbone lights up the face of a fairy princess (opposite).

Color can arouse emotions; fear is suggested by the eerie green look of this witch face.

Animal faces, like this lion's, often have a split upper lip connected to a dark nose.

Index

Cowles Creative Publishing, Inc.
offers a variety of how-to books. For
information write:
  Cowles Creative Publishing
  Subscriber Books
  5900 Green Oak Drive
  Minnetonka, MN 55343